LUCY'S BAKES

OVER 200 OF THE EASIEST BAKING RECIPES YOU WILL EVER MAKE

LUCY CUFFLIN

WITH LUCY LEE-TIRRELL

For Ian, a true cake lover

LUCY'S BAKES

OVER 200 OF THE EASIEST BAKING RECIPES YOU WILL EVER MAKE

LUCY CUFFLIN

WITH LUCY LEE-TIRRELL

FEATURING TESTER NOTES FROM REAL-LIFE HOME BAKERS

hardie grant books
MELBOURNE · LONDON

CONTENTS

INTRODUCTION
Page 7

CAKES
CHAPTER 1, *Page 23*

COOKIES AND BISCUITS
CHAPTER 2, *Page 67*

SWEET TREATS
CHAPTER 3, *Page 83*

TRAYBAKES
CHAPTER 4, *Page 103*

BREAD
CHAPTER 5, *Page 131*

SAVOURY
CHAPTER 6, *Page 159*

FESTIVE TREATS
CHAPTER 7, *Page 173*

TOPPINGS AND FILLINGS
CHAPTER 8, *Page 191*

ACKNOWLEDGEMENTS
Page 200

ABOUT THE AUTHOR
Page 201

INDEX
Page 202

INTRODUCTION

When my publishers asked me to write a second cook book, this time all about baking, I asked myself 'What can I tell people about baking that hasn't already been said?' Well, here's the thing… I have planned, created, collated and coordinated menus and recipes for ski chalets for 14 years. In each of the 110 Skiworld chalets I work with, afternoon tea is served every single day and that's a lot of teas – something like a quarter of a million in the season! All of the traybakes, cookies and treats have to work every time for all the staff, whatever their baking know-how. They always tell me that if the recipe only uses one bowl then that's an added bonus so that is what I have always tried to do – hone, trim and simplify so there is less to go wrong and usually less washing up at the end! This has meant that I believe I can understand what makes the difference between a good recipe and a fabulous foolproof recipe. It's not about quick fixes or time saving for the sake of it, it's about testing 100 tips to find the three that really make the difference. About removing unnecessary cooking steps but holding onto the ones that make sure the result is still perfect. It is about uncomplicating cooking while hopefully adding a little magic along the way.

I always think of baking as the friendly side of cooking. It is not something we often do to sustain life or just to feed ourselves, it is about enjoyment and is often quite a social form of cooking. So this was not a book to write by myself; instead I teamed up with my oldest cooking chum, 'the other Lucy' (or, to avoid confusion, Lucy LT as she signs her e-mails). We pooled recipes and we baked liked we'd never baked before – and we loved every waist-busting minute of it! But there really is only so much cake you can eat and, as baking is all about sharing, that is exactly what we did. We roped in friends, family and colleagues to road-test the recipes and as an added bonus, our team of road-testers came back with additions and variations we had not imagined. So, a really big 'thank you' to everyone who donned an apron and flourished a wooden spoon in aid of this book.

But don't think that our baking is all doilies and cake stands. There is something deeply fulfilling about being elbow-deep in bread flour or making a wonderful mess in the kitchen cooking with the children. So from dainty afternoon tea to the slab of fruitcake when out on a hike, it's all here – simple, achievable and enjoyable. Get your bowl at the ready and start baking – share the love and feed the soul.

BEFORE YOU START COOKING — TIPS AND TRICKS FOR SUCCESSFUL BAKING

- If you only read one tip this is it: read the whole recipe before you start, top to bottom. It sounds so simple but hardly anyone does it and most mistakes are made because they didn't – so do!

- There are tips and notes on each recipe from the testers so read what they have to say. There are some inspirational variations on the recipes too.

- See the notes on buying ingredients on page 12 and notes on buying equipment on page 11.

- Invest in a set of digital scales (or get them on your birthday list) so you can weigh everything more easily. Put the mixing bowl on the scales and zero it between adding different ingredients – less fuss, less mess. See tips on buying scales on page 11.

- Invest in a set of proper measuring spoons. Your teaspoon may be a world away from a technical teaspoon. See notes on page 11.

- I measure liquid in grams not millilitres so I can weigh them on my digital scales (easier and less washing up). However, if you don't have digital scales, you can use millilitres instead – they are interchangeable (so if I say 250 g (9 oz) water, you can use 250 ml (9 fl oz)).

GETTING TO KNOW YOUR OVEN

- In 30 years of cooking in many different kitchens I have yet to find an oven that behaves perfectly. So take a bit of time to get to know your oven, follow the tips below and it will save you heartache on a day when you just need your baking to be right first time.

- If you have a gas oven, the temperature will be hotter at the top than the bottom. The set temperature is for cooking food on the shelf just above the centre so if you need to put several trays of bakes in the oven at the same time on shelves one above the other, you may need to swap them around halfway through cooking to get even baking. I prefer to cook in batches so I get perfect results and don't have to keep opening the oven door but that, of course, uses more fuel, so the choice is yours.

- I always use an electric fan oven as I find I get better results. If you have one, use it and reduce the temperatures in the book as in the chart opposite:

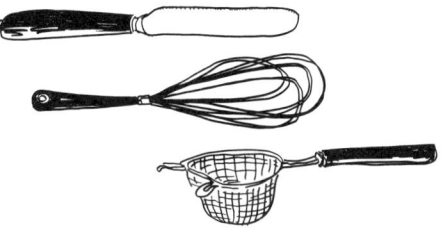

8 LUCY'S BAKES

°C	°F	Gas	Fan °C
110	230	¼	90
120	250	½	100
140	275	1	120
150	300	2	130
160	320	3	140
180	350	4	160
190	375	5	170
200	400	6	180
220	430	7	200
230	450	8	210
240	475	9	220

TROUBLESHOOTING

Here are some common baking problems.

- **ALL MY BAKING TAKES LONGER THAN THE SUGGESTED RECIPE TIME**
  Buy an oven thermometer and it will probably show you that your oven is not quite coming to the temperature you set. So test what temperature you need to set the dial to get the internal temperature you want and follow that in all recipes.

- **CAKES ARE BROWNING BEFORE THEY ARE COOKED**
  Then the oven is probably getting hotter than the dial indicates, so do the same as above and reduce the dial temperature for future baking.

- **MY CAKES BROWN ON THE TOP BEFORE THEY ARE COOKED**
  Put the cake on a lower shelf and place a baking sheet on the wire shelf above the cake.

- **MY CAKES BURN UNDERNEATH**
  Put the cake on a higher shelf and place a baking sheet on the shelf below to shield the cake from the fierce bottom element.

- **ONE SIDE BAKES DARKER THAN THE OTHER**
  Your oven is not circulating the heat evenly and you can remedy this in any cooking by turning the cake tray or tin halfway through cooking. BUT beware with cakes as if you open the oven too early you run the risk of the cake sinking. So my advice is wait until three-quarters of the way through cooking then turn the cake on the shelf without removing it – if that is possible – so you reduce the drop in temperature and don't disturb the cake too much.

BAKING FOR ALLERGY SUFFERERS

LACTOSE INTOLERANT

This is an easy allergy to cater for when baking because there are many lactose-free products around. We love the lactofree range by Arla who produce everything from butter, cream cheese and hard cheese to milk and cream substitutes. The flavours are wonderful and the fats seem to work really well in cakes and cookies alike. There are other makes of fats and cheeses but take a look at this range.

COELIAC (CELIAC) OR GLUTEN INTOLERANT/ WHEAT INTOLERANT

Wheat, barley and rye flours all contain gluten – a protein which can cause an allergic reaction. Most supermarkets and health food shops now do good gluten-free flour blends for baking. They are intended to substitute measure for measure with ordinary baking flours. We love the Doves Farm flour blends for baking but try other brands and experiment. What I would say, though, is that most gluten-free flour blends need a little extra liquid in the recipe so I tend to add a couple of tablespoons of water to whatever I am baking – experimentation is the key, find a make you like and stick to it. Most of the recipes here will work if you tweak them this way a little. Doves Farm also does a range of bread flours and a very good fast-action dried yeast.

There is some controversy about oats and gluten. Oats themselves do not contain gluten but a similar protein and some sufferers still get a reaction from it. Also, not all oats are gluten-free because they have been milled in a factory with gluten products and therefore have residual wheat in them. So always check the label that they are certified gluten-free if necessary. You also need to check your baking powder as not all are gluten-free.

People with a wheat intolerance can eat rye, barley and oats. However, read the labels if buying rye bread as it is often combined with wheat flour to give a lighter texture.

NUT ALLERGIES

Nuts fall into two categories: ground nuts and tree nuts. Ground nuts include peanuts, which are the most common nut for nut allergies. However, some people who are allergic to peanuts can happily eat tree nuts, such as almonds, walnuts and pecans. Some people are also allergic to seeds. In this book, nuts and seeds, for the most part, are an extra to the recipe so can be omitted. So, for instance, if you want to make the Florentine Bars on page 115 and you cannot use nuts, simply load the top with dried fruit (and seeds if you can tolerate them). All recipes in the book with no added nuts or seeds are marked as nut-free. Also check the labels of any ready-made product you may use for nut content – mayonnaise, packaged sweets etc.

TIPS ON BUYING EQUIPMENT

- The tins I use the most are a 20 cm (8 in) round, deep cake tin with a loose bottom, a 20 cm (8 in) square cake tin for traybakes and cakes and a larger 20 x 30 cm (8 x 12 in) shallow traybake tin. I occasionally use a 25 cm (10 in) diameter shallower cake tin and I have two favourite baking sheets that I use all the time. I love enamel-coated baking tins – they are almost invincible and good baking tins can last a lifetime. So whichever finish you prefer, it is well worth spending a bit on them as they can stay with you for a while.

- If you choose to buy digital scales then make sure you buy scales that can weigh up to 5 kg (11 lb) top weight; this will allow you to use a large mixing bowl and still weigh successfully. A medium-priced scale will also measure very small amounts successfully.

- If you buy one piece of equipment only I would buy an electric hand whisk. There are many on the market and you do not need to spend a fortune, but an electric whisk will save you a lot of arm-ache. I have a hand blender for blending and grinding nuts and I have an electric whisk for beating cake mixture and whisking egg whites. The electric whisk would be my first purchase and a hand blender would be my second.

- If you are hooked on baking then get a fixed-head mixer on your Christmas list. Don't be tempted by inexpensive models as they tend not to be very robust – save up and buy something solid. I have had my KitchenAid for 25 years and it is as good as the day I bought it. My mother had her Kenwood Chef for over 30 years. There are other makes on the market but I would search out one with a steel body.

- Measuring spoons come in all shapes and materials. My favourite set I own are magnetic and sit inside each other then magnetise to my knife rack. You can choose a set that suits you but look for a ¼ teaspoon to tablespoon measurement range.

- A spatula is a baker's friend, making sure all your lovely cake mixture ends up in the tin. There are fabulous ones that are heat resistant, moulded in a single piece (so no joins) and available in colours to match your kitchen – whichever type you choose this is a tool I could not live without.

- I inherited my mother's palette knife that she had when she married. It is over 50 years old. It's one of the best tools I have. A palette knife is really useful for spreading icing (frosting) or cake mix or 100 other jobs. Buy a good one as it may outlive you.

- Piping can make your topping look really professional. Disposable piping bags are in most supermarkets but you can also buy them online. In many shops they only sell very small piping nozzles so buy one large fluted-end nozzle from either a specialist baking shop or online. I prefer disposable bags to washable piping bags because I find that the flavours linger in the cloth over time. One of my least favourite jobs in the kitchen is washing the piping bag. I rarely use one to be honest so I keep a store of disposable ones to hand.

- A heavy-based saucepan is good for heating sugar to prevent burning. I have stainless steel pans from a well-known Swedish shop that have bases that are quite adequate, so no need to search out a specialist pan.

- Dishwasher-safe silicone spoons, spatulas and tools are a great asset as they do not warp or trap bits of food in joins.

GLOSSARY OF INGREDIENTS AND BUYING TIPS

- **BAKING POWDER** – a mix of bicarbonate of soda (baking soda) and cream of tartar. This is an ideal mix of ingredients to make a cake rise, but use bicarbonate on its own where called for in some cookie recipes, as it is this that gives them that crinkly top.

- **BALSAMIC VINEGAR** – required for the Fast Balsamic Syrup on page 193, this can be any brand as you are adding the flavours *and* sugar so no need to spend heavily on the basic commodity.

- **BANANAS** – when using bananas for cake-baking, buy ripe ones or let yours ripen before using. Underripe bananas will give a chewy texture and not much flavour. You can use them even if the skins have gone black.

- **CARDAMOM PODS** – available in most supermarkets but online you can buy the seeds already removed from the husk.

- **CHESTNUT PURÉE** – readily available in cans in most supermarkets.

- **CHILLI FLAKES** – not the same as chilli powder, these are little flakes of dried chilli as the name suggests. Gram for gram these are less hot than chilli powder as they are less condensed. They are available in most supermarkets and Asian grocery stores.

- **CHOCOLATE** – the ideal dark chocolate for baking would be anything around the 50 per cent cocoa solids and there are many brands that offer this. I find that 70 per cent cocoa solids is sometimes too bitter for some recipes so not necessarily a treat. Milk chocolate is much sweeter and there are recipes that ask for it particularly – mostly you can use dark if you prefer or blend the two for a medium cocoa taste. White chocolate is not really chocolate and contain no cocoa solids but contains cocoa butter. It melts differently so be careful if you melt it in the microwave as it burns easily. It is best to do this in a bowl over a pan of boiling water but don't let the bowl touch the water, don't overheat and don't stir or it will solidify!

- **CHOCOLATE SPREAD** – for baking and icing cakes. Buy your favourite brand with or without hazelnuts.

- **COCOA POWDER** – do not confuse this with hot chocolate powder. Hot chocolate powder is cocoa powder with added sugar and sometimes milk powder. This will make you recipe very sweet and not chocolatey enough. Pure cocoa powder is the best – many brands are pure, just check the ingredients label.

- **CONDENSED MILK** – do not confuse this with evaporated milk. Condensed milk is a sweet, thick-textured liquid of concentrated sweetened milk. We caramelise in the tin in some recipes or you can buy it ready caramelised – it simply says 'caramel' on the milk tin.

- **COLOURED GLACÉ CHERRIES** – available from some good supermarkets, online or from specialist baking shops.

- **CORNMEAL** – cornmeal is very fine. Some of the bread recipes will work with coarser meal like polenta but the cakes really need fine cornmeal. You can buy it online or find it in the Caribbean section of a supermarket – you many need to buy a large bag but it is very inexpensive and it keeps well in a cool, dark place.

- **CRYSTALLISED GINGER** – can be found in the baking section of most supermarkets. It is cut into about 1 cm (½ in) chunks and coated in sugar. Usually you will need to chop this a bit smaller to use in baking.

- **DATES** – can be bought in many ways but we avoid the ready chopped dates as they are often sugar-coated and can be dry. Ready-stoned dates are a bonus as stoning can take a while. Having said that, some of the natural dates with stones are some of the most succulent I have eaten. If I am making the High-Energy Date Bars (see page 129) then I prefer to stone my own as they are a big part of the flavour.

- **EDIBLE ROSE PETALS** – the easiest way to buy these is online. They are light, so cost little to post, and you can purchase other floral ingredients at the same time.

- **EGGS** – a normal size egg in a cake recipe will weigh approximately 60 g (2 oz) including shell. If your eggs are a great deal larger then adjust the other ingredients accordingly. It can make a real difference to the end result. Eggs with really yellow yolks will give your baking a healthy yellowy colour which can be really beautiful.

- **ESSENCES AND EXTRACTS** – it is well worth buying the natural extracts, as there is a world of difference in flavour between the natural extract and the chemical essence. We love vanilla pastes and extracts that contain the seeds.

- **FENNEL SEEDS** – available in most good supermarkets with the herbs and spices, or in larger quantities in the Asian or foreign food sections, or from Asian grocery stores or online.

- **FLOUR** – you can choose own brand, organic stone milled and anything in between, but use the flour asked for by the recipe. Use strong bread flour for the breads as cake flour simply does not work and use what we might refer to as ordinary flour for cakes and biscuits. Self-raising flour is plain (all-purpose) flour with baking powder added. Rye and spelt flour is widely available these days and you can make your own oat flour/meal by blending porridge oats to a flour consistency.

- **GLUTEN-FREE FLOUR BLENDS** – see notes on Baking For Allergy Sufferers on page 10, but many makes now offer a gluten-free flour blend that is excellent for baking. It is a blend of many pulses and grains that are gluten-free but offer a good texture for cakes and biscuits. We like the Doves Farm brand.

- **GOLDEN SYRUP** – I use Lyle's golden syrup because it is made from sugar cane. Many own brands are made from sugar beet and they lack the flavour sugar cane syrup has.

- **GROUND GINGER** – look in the Asian cooking aisle of the supermarket or any Asian grocery store for this as it is cheaper and often a much hotter ginger than the one found in small jars on the herbs/spice aisle in most supermarkets.

- **HONEY** – as huge fans we can recommend local honey but it may be that your local honey does not have the flavour you are after. If the main source of pollen for the bees is rape flower then the honey flavour can be very mild, so it's worth searching out specific ones for baking such as lavender honeys, floral honeys or even some branded honeys which can have rich, earthy flavours.

- **LAVENDER** – pick from your garden at the end of summer, tie in a bunch and allow to dry, then take the flowers off the stalks and store in a screw-topped jar. Alternatively you can buy ready-dried washed lavender online (try www.justingredients.co.uk for a large selection of spices and dried flowers). You can add them to many recipes, but try the Honey Lavender Flapjack on page 125.

- **MARZIPAN** – available in white or yellow in most supermarkets or speciality food stores. Some dedicated cake decorating shops will sell it in various other colours.

- **MAYONNAISE** – for baking where we have asked for mayonnaise we have used Hellmann's. This has 8 per cent egg content. If your brand has less than this, add an extra tablespoon to the recipe.

- **ONION SEEDS** – sometimes called nigella or kalonji seeds, these are available from most supermarkets, online or from any Asian grocer.

- **PASSION FRUIT** – can be found in most supermarkets or greengrocers. The outside does not give away the brightly coloured yellow seedy pulp inside. All the recipes that call for passion fruit use the seeds and pulp together.

- **POPPY SEEDS** – available in most supermarkets in the baking section.

- **STEM GINGER** – available from some supermarkets and speciality food stores. It is whole glacé root ginger in syrup. The ginger is fabulously strong-flavoured but sweet and the syrup is great for drizzling over cakes and muffins.

- **SUGAR** – I use caster (superfine) sugar for most recipes and golden caster has a better flavour than pure white, refined caster but the choice is yours. Occasionally I use soft brown or demerara (raw) sugar for flavour or texture. Granulated is good for jams and syrups. I like white icing (confectioners') sugar for my toppings – you can buy golden icing sugar but I think this gives all toppings a sort of beige hue.

- **WHOLE ALMONDS** – come blanched (no skin) or unblanched, with a brown skin. Use either but if you want a more refined look, buy the blanched ones. I think the unblanched almonds have a better flavour.

- **YEAST** – fresh yeast is available in a few supermarkets in the chilled section near fresh pastry and butter. As my bread recipes are intended to be store cupboard bakes, I use fast-action dried yeast. This is different from ordinary dried yeast as it needs no presoaking or mixing. It can be stirred into the dry ingredients and you can get straight on with the kneading and shaping of the dough. I have sometimes given you the option for fresh yeast, if you prefer.

MEET THE TESTERS

Starting out on this book, Lucy LT and I soon realised that we needed more mouths to test our recipes. Luckily, after a few calls we had an army of friends and colleagues ready to take the bakes through their paces. What we hadn't anticipated was the wonderful variations that this team of testers would offer us – what they added or did differently to make the recipe 'theirs'. We've included these, so not only do you get the knowledge that the original recipe has been tried, tested, baked and loved, but you also get some inspirational variations to try! A huge thanks to this team of enthusiastic testers and we hope you enjoy reading their comments along the way.

SARA MCDONALD HAS SPENT THE PAST FIVE YEARS MANAGING SKI CHALETS AND RESORTS IN THE FRENCH ALPS. SHE IS A HUGE FAN OF ASIAN CUISINE AND IN HER SPARE TIME LOVES DANCING.

LIKES
GALAXY CHOCOLATE, ASIAN FOOD, ROAST DINNERS.

DISLIKES
BANANAS, TOMATOES, CUCUMBER.

GEMMA HEDGES HAS BEEN COOKING CUPCAKES WITH HER NAN SINCE SHE WAS LITTLE. SHE HAS BEEN WORKING IN SKI CHALETS AND HOTELS FOR SIX YEARS AND HAS BAKED MANY, MANY AFTERNOON TEA CAKES!

LIKES
CHEESE, OLIVES, CHOCOLATE.

DISLIKES
AUBERGINES (EGGPLANT), PINE NUTS, MARZIPAN.

DI PALUMBO IS THE SALES AND MARKETING DIRECTOR AT SKIWORLD. DI HAS SPENT MANY YEARS IN THE SKI INDUSTRY. 'I EXERCISE A LOT SO I CAN EAT GOOD FOOD WITHOUT FEELING GUILTY', SHE SAYS.

LIKES
FOOD WITH FLAVOUR, SCALLOPS, HOMEMADE PASTA.

DISLIKES
APRICOTS, RAW CELERY, OVERCOOKED FISH.

BRENDAN CROFT IS ORIGINALLY FROM AUSTRALIA AND LOVES TO TRAVEL, EAT FINE FOOD, DRINK NICE WINE AND CRAFT BEERS. HE IS A SELF-CONFESSED COFFEE SNOB AND A CYCLING ADDICT.

LIKES
SMOKED BBQ MEATS, SPICY FOOD, TIRAMISU.

DISLIKES
MUSHROOMS, BEETROOT (BEETS), BRUSSELS SPROUTS.

PENNY VICKERS LIVES IN LEICESTER AND HAS ENJOYED TESTING THE RECIPES AND FEEDING THEM TO HUSBAND MIKE AND THE LEICESTER RUGBY TIGER CLUB LODGER.

LIKES
TURNIPS, SPINACH, CREAM.

DISLIKES
WHEAT, WINE, CUSTARD.

ELLA ARGENTIER IS AT COLLEGE IN GRENOBLE AND ENJOYS BAKING. SHE PARTICULARLY LIKES CAKES WITH TEXTURES SO IS ALWAYS ADDING BITS AND BOBS TO RECIPES. ELLA ALSO LIKES TO INVENT SALADS AND ENJOYS COOKING WITH PASTA.

LIKES
LIGHT, FRESH AND FLAVOURSOME FOOD THAT IS WELL PRESENTED.

DISLIKES
FATTY, RICH FOODS.

KERRY GREGORY IS A BUSY MUM WITH FOUR CHILDREN AND A HUSBAND TO CATER FOR. SHE IS A VEGETARIAN, AS IS HER DAUGHTER, AND HAS A VERY FUSSY TODDLER. ALL THE CHILDREN ENJOY BAKING – ESPECIALLY MAKING FRESH BREAD.

LIKES
OPHELIA: BISCUITS, CAKES, CHILLIES, NUTS. **RUPERT:** SPINACH, FISH FINGERS. **OLIVER:** EGGS, BAKED BEANS. **FELIX:** MARSHMALLOWS, WATERMELON.

DISLIKES
OPHELIA: MEAT, BANANAS. **RUPERT:** AVOCADOS, EGGS. **OLIVER:** CHILLIES, HAMBURGERS. **FELIX:** SALAD, PEANUT BUTTER.

FIONA GALLAGHER AND OLLIE EVANS MET IN ST. ANTON IN 2011 AND HAVE BEEN SNOWBOARDING, TRAVELLING AND COOKING TOGETHER EVER SINCE. THEY HAVE RECENTLY MOVED TO QUEENSTOWN, NEW ZEALAND BECAUSE OF FIONA'S LOVE OF THE 'LORD OF THE RINGS' MOVIES AND PLAN TO STAY THERE FOR THE FORESEEABLE FUTURE.

LIKES
FIONA AND OLLIE: HEARTY AUSTRIAN FOOD, DELICATE BUT SPICY THAI FOOD AND TAPAS.

DISLIKES
FIONA AND OLLIE: PROCESSED, PREMADE AND BORING FOOD!

JANET MEEKCOMS GREW UP EATING HOME-GROWN AND HOME-BAKED FOOD; EATING OUT WAS VISITING GRANDPARENTS AND THE ONLY FAST-FOOD WAS FISH AND CHIPS. HER LATE HUSBAND, FRED, WHOSE MOTHER WAS A FANTASTIC COOK, PASSED ON A LOVE OF FOOD AND COOKING TO THEIR SONS AND GRANDSONS.

LIKES
FISH (ESPECIALLY DOVER SOLE), CHEESES (STRONG CHEDDAR, SAINT FÉLICIEN, STILTON), CRÈME BRÛLÉE.

DISLIKES
MEAT (ENCOURAGED BY A VEGETARIAN FATHER), TAPIOCA PUDDING, COCONUT.

LYDIA CUFFLIN AND SIMON CHILDS ARE BOTH FOODIES; LYDIA'S GRANNY ENSURED THAT SHE COULD MAKE (AND EAT) A MERINGUE BEFORE SHE COULD WALK. SIMON WAS AN EATER NOT A COOK, BUT AFTER A SKI SEASON, HE CAN NOW HOLD HIS OWN IN THE KITCHEN. THEY LOVE TO COOK FOR FRIENDS AND FAMILY.

LIKES
LYDIA: ALL CHEESES, GIN AND TONIC, OLIVES.
SIMON: CHOC-CHIP COOKIES, BACON, PEANUT BUTTER.

DISLIKES
LYDIA: CHICKEN, NUT ROAST, WAFER BISCUITS.
SIMON: BLUE CHEESE, JAM, HOT DRINKS.

BEN COLEBY STUDIED MUSIC AT UNIVERSITY BUT ON LEAVING FOLLOWED HIS PASSION FOR FOOD AND TRAINED AS A CHEF. HE LOVES JAPANESE FOOD, AND HAS WORKED AT A TOP-END SUSHI RESTAURANT AND IZAKAYA PUB IN LONDON, AND IS NOW MANAGING SEVERAL SKI CHALETS IN THE ALPS.

LIKES
MUSHROOMS, OYSTERS, AVOCADO.

DISLIKES
PASSION FRUIT, TURKEY, SMOOTHIES.

MAURICE FLYNN SAYS, 'I USED TO BE A CAKE ADDICT, AND HAVE TRIED TO OVERCOME THIS ADDICTION BY BECOMING A PUSHER'. MAURICE IS OFTEN UP TO HIS ELBOWS IN CAKE BATTER, STILL TRYING TO PERFECT HIS MOTHERS RICH AND FRUITY IRISH TEA BRACK.

LIKES
GINGER, CHERRIES, DARK MARMALADE.

DISLIKES
PICCALILLI, BREAD AND BUTTER PUDDING, RUNNY SCRAMBLED EGGS.

MARCELLA SCOTT IS A KEEN SURFER AND SNOWBOARDER. SHE HAS SPENT 10 WINTERS MANAGING CHALETS IN THE FRENCH ALPS AND IS CURRENTLY BAKING AND SERVING CAKES IN A CORNISH TEA ROOM.

LIKES
KANGAROO STEAK, AVOCADO, RED WINE.

DISLIKES
ASPARAGUS, TOMATOES, BANANAS.

HELEN WOOLDRIDGE HAS DONE FOUR WINTER SEASONS IN VARIOUS RESORTS IN THE ALPS. SHE LOVES TRAVELLING AND TASTING FOOD FROM ALL OVER THE WORLD. SHE ENJOYS RECREATING THE DISHES SHE FOUND ON HER TRAVELS TO SERVE TO HER GUESTS IN THE CHALET.

LIKES
CHOCOLATE, CHEESE, COFFEE.

DISLIKES
BACON, HAM, SALAMI.

LIZ EVERSON COOKS A LOT OF ASIAN FOOD AT HOME BECAUSE SHE LOVES THE FLAVOURS AND GREW UP EATING CURRY. SHE LIKES COOKING FOR FRIENDS BUT HASN'T BAKED SINCE SHE WAS A TEENAGER UNTIL TESTING THE RECIPES FOR THIS BOOK.

LIKES ALL SAVOURY FOOD, ESPECIALLY FRENCH AND INDIAN; A CHEESEBOARD.

DISLIKES PIZZA, PASTA, SWEET FOODS.

RUTH HULME IS A KEEN HOME COOK WHO LOVES NOTHING MORE THAN BAKING FOR FRIENDS, FAMILY AND COLLEAGUES. RUTH HAS AN ALLOTMENT WHERE SHE GROWS PRODUCE TO MAKE PICKLES, CHUTNEYS AND MARMALADE FROM HER GRANDMA'S SECRET RECIPES.

LIKES CHEESE, MARMITE, BEEF.

DISLIKES SALMON, PINEAPPLE, BROCCOLI.

NAOMI HULME HAS BEEN WORKING IN SKI RESORTS FOR OVER 15 YEARS. SHE LOVES COOKING AND DEVELOPS, TESTS AND WRITES THE MENU PLANS THAT ARE SERVED IN 120 CHALETS THROUGH FRANCE, SWITZERLAND AND AUSTRIA.

LIKES CELERY, PORK BELLY, RASPBERRIES.

DISLIKES SHELLFISH, ICE CREAM, MUSHROOMS.

JOVANKA BJELIC LOVES GOOD FOOD BUT HER HUSBAND DOES MOST OF THE COOKING IN THEIR BUSY HOUSEHOLD. ORIGINALLY FROM SERBIA, THEY COOK MOSTLY TRADITIONAL RECIPES AT HOME AND LOVED TESTING SOME NEW RECIPES FROM THE BOOK.

LIKES MERINGUES, ROAST CHICKEN, HOMEMADE FOOD.

DISLIKES LIQUORICE, HOT CHILLIES.

RON SAWERS, A RETIRED BANKER, HAS BEEN A COMITTED HOUSE HUSBAND TO HIS WIFE AND TWIN BOYS. HE IS A KEEN GARDENER AND SOMEWHAT RELUCTANT (BUT ENTHUSIASTIC) HOME COOK.

LIKES ROAST BEEF, FISH AND CHIPS, SALADS (NICOISE, GREEK AND CAESAR).

DISLIKES COUSCOUS, MOST INDIAN FOOD, 'BONEY' FISH.

IRENE O'SULLIVAN AND JENNY GREENWOOD HEAD UP THE RECRUITMENT DEPARTMENT AT SKIWORLD AND ARE PASSIONATE ABOUT FOOD. ALL THEIR CHALET HOST APPLICANTS BRING IN A CAKE THEY HAVE MADE TO DEMONSTRATE THEIR COOKING SKILLS, SO THEY ARE ALSO GREAT CAKE TASTERS!

LIKES DARK CHOCOLATE, CHEESE, AVOCADOS.

DISLIKES RED MEAT, TURKISH DELIGHT, ANCHOVIES.

HATTIE CUFFLIN IS AN EVENTS MANAGEMENT GRADUATE WHO LOVES TO BAKE! AT 21 SHE DOESN'T REMEMBER A BIRTHDAY WHERE SHE DIDN'T MAKE HER OWN CAKE. 'WHEN I'M NOT IN THE KITCHEN I'LL EITHER BE RELAXING OR BROWSING FOR MY NEXT RECIPE.'

LIKES WINE, CHEESE, CHOCOLATE.

DISLIKES PRAWNS, MUSHROOMS, COFFEE.

SAMUEL RAFTER HAS FOLLOWED HIS PASSION FOR COFFEE AND IS WORKING AS A BARISTA FOR ARTISAN COFFEE IN LONDON. SAMUEL LOVES SKIING AND IS A DEDICATED FOODIE. HE KEEPS FIT AT THE GYM AND ON HIS LONGBOARD.

LIKES GOOD COFFEE, CARPACCIO OF BEEF, PASTA.

DISLIKES TURKISH DELIGHT, DARK CHOCOLATE, PRUNES.

IAN COLEBY, FOUNDER AND CHAIRMAN OF SKIWORLD LTD. IN RECENT YEARS HE HAS DEVELOPED A LOVE FOR THE ALPS IN THE SUMMER MONTHS HIKING. HE IS A KEEN CYCLIST AND A COMPLETE BAKING NOVICE WHEN HE BEGAN TESTING RECIPES FOR THE BOOK!

LIKES REAL ALE, OYSTERS, PORK BELLY.

DISLIKES LAGER, ONIONS, WHITE CHOCOLATE.

ANTONIA ARGENTIER IS A TEACHER IN GRENOBLE. SHE HAS THREE CHILDREN AT HOME AND HAS A BUSY LIFE. SHE ENJOYS SPORT, RUNNING AND A GLASS OF GOOD WINE WITH FRIENDS.

LIKES
OYSTERS, CRISPY CRUNCHY SALADS, DISCOVERING NEW LOCAL SPECIALITIES.

DISLIKES
SLIPPERY FRIED EGGS, COOKED CHEESE, BLAND FOOD.

JO CURD LOVES WALKING, READING AND SEEING FRIENDS. SHE IS CO-FOUNDER OF AUTISTIC EYE LTD., AND WORKS IN SCHOOLS.

LIKES
MIDDLE EASTERN FOOD, SPAGHETTI, OLIVES.

DISLIKES
MOST OFFAL, TOMATO KETCHUP, GHERKINS.

JOSH CURD RUNS A SMALL ENTERPRISE CALLED AUTISTIC EYE LTD. HIS PASSIONS INCLUDE BOARD GAMES, COMPUTER GAMES, MUSIC AND OWLS. **BEN CURD** IS A FREELANCE MUSIC VIDEO PRODUCER, WHO ENJOYS LONGBOARDING AND PLAYING BASS AND ACOUSTIC GUITAR.

LIKES
JOSH: HOT SPICY FOOD, JAPANESE FOOD, PULLED PORK.
BEN: ROAST BEEF, YORKSHIRE PUDDING, GRAVY.

DISLIKES
JOSH: ORANGES, BAMBOO SHOOTS.
BEN: SARDINES, ONIONS, SOFT APPLES.

IAN MEEKCOMS WORKS MOST HOURS AS A CARPENTER, WHILE HIS WIFE **ANNETTE MEEKCOMS** IS A SECRETARY WHO SPENDS A LOT OF TIME FERRYING THEIR SONS AROUND. AS A FAMILY THEY ENJOY EATING OUT AT THEIR LOCAL TURKISH RESTAURANT.

LIKES
IAN AND ANNETTE: A GOOD BARBECUE, TARTIFLETTE, SEAFOOD, MONKFISH.

DISLIKES
IAN: ANYTHING WITH GOATS' MILK!
ANNETTE: PEAS AND MUSHROOMS.

JACK MEEKCOMS, ENJOYS KARATE, SKIING AND SKATEBOARDING. **TOBY MEEKCOMS** LIKES FOOD, ESPECIALLY CORNED BEEF! HE ALSO ENJOYS KARATE AND OUTDOOR ACTIVITIES WITH THE CUBS.

LIKES
JACK: STEAK
TOBY: CHICKEN, CORNED BEEF, CAKE.

DISLIKES
JACK: LAMB
TOBY: CHEESE

STELLA CAUDWELL LOVED TO BAKE CAKES AND PUDDINGS AS A TEENAGER. NOW RECENTLY RETIRED FROM A CAREER IN THE FOOD INDUSTRY SHE IS REDISCOVERING HOW SATISFYING IT IS TO BAKE!

LIKES
HOTEL BREAKFAST, HOMEMADE GRAVY, GOOD-QUALITY COFFEE.

DISLIKES
LOW-FAT SNACKS, MAYO.

CATHERINE AND MATTHEW SELLS CATHERINE LIVES AND WORKS IN THE RURAL HEART OF STAFFORDSHIRE WITH HER HUSBAND, HER SON MATTHEW AND THEIR DOGS, PIGS, DUCKS, HENS AND SHEEP.

LIKES
CATHERINE: SPICY VEG, ROAST PORK BELLY, GOATS' CHEESE.
MATTHEW: ALL FRUIT, MUSSELS, HARIBO.

DISLIKES
CATHERINE AND MATTHEW: MELON BALLS, PINEAPPLE ON PIZZA, ANYTHING WITH KIDNEY.

HARRY ROGERS LIKES UNICYCLING AND PLAYING THE PIANO AND **MIA ROGERS** LOVES FOOD AND IS LEARNING HOW TO KNIT.

LIKES
HARRY: TROUT, SAUSAGES, CHEESECAKE.
MIA: DOVER SOLE, PORK PIE, SALAD.

DISLIKES
HARRY: COOKED CARROTS, CHILLIES, POTATOES.
MIA: PEAS, CHICKEN IN BREADCRUMBS.

HANNAH, AJ AND MADDY CUFFLIN LIVE IN LEICESTERSHIRE WITH MUM AND DAD AND BROTHER MICHAEL. HANNAH LOVES ATHLETICS AND COMPETES REGULARLY WHILE AJ JUST LOVES TO DANCE.

LIKES
ICE CREAM, PEANUT BUTTER, CHOCOLATE, SAUSAGES, SPAGHETTI.

DISLIKES
CABBAGE, BOVRIL, LASAGNE, BRUSSELS SPROUTS.

MICHAEL CUFFLIN LOVES TO BAKE AND IN HIS SPARE TIME HE PLAYS TENNIS, TENNIS AND MORE TENNIS.

LIKES
CAKE, CHICKEN, PIE.

DISLIKES
BEETROOT (BEETS), BRUSSELS SPROUTS, TUNA.

TOM ROBERTS' GREATEST ACHIEVEMENT IS FIRST PRIZE FOR HIS CHEESE STRAWS IN THE LOCAL PRODUCE SHOW IN 2013. HIS GREATEST DISAPPOINTMENT WAS COMING SECOND TO HIS BEST FRIEND THE FOLLOWING YEAR!

LIKES
MAKING PIES, EATING PIES.

DISLIKES
PIES THAT DO NOT HAVE PASTRY TOP AND BOTTOM.

CLAIRE VAN DIJK WORKED AS A COOK FOR MANY YEARS AND AS A BAKER FOR LUCY'S FOOD. SHE LIVES IN LEICESTER WITH HER HUSBAND AND HAS TWO GROWN-UP DAUGHTERS AND A TEENAGE SON. SHE LOVES FOOD AND SIMPLY ADORES TO BAKE.

LIKES
UNUSUAL FLAVOURS, ESPECIALLY FLORAL.

DISLIKES
BLAND AND BADLY COOKED FOOD, CHINESE.

KAJAL MISTRY IS THE SENIOR EDITOR OF HARDIE GRANT BOOKS. WHEN SHE'S NOT EDITING COOK BOOKS SHE'S TESTING OUT HER CULINARY SKILLS IN THE KITCHEN. FOOD IS PRETTY MUCH ALWAYS ON HER MIND!

LIKES
LENTILS, AUBERGINE (EGGPLANT), SPICES, SEAFOOD, SPINACH, OLIVES, EGGS, CHILLI OIL, SALTED CARAMEL, TIRAMISU.

DISLIKES
MARZIPAN, PINEAPPLE ON PIZZA, LIQUORICE ALLSORTS, ALCO POPS, FIZZY DRINKS.

MARK SCILLEY HAS LIVED IN FRANCE FOR OVER 30 YEARS. HE STARTED BAKING THIS YEAR FOR THE FIRST TIME SINCE HE WAS A CHILD. HE LOVES WALKING IN THE NATIONAL PARK ON HIS DOORSTEP.

LIKES
WINE, LOCALLY GROWN AND MEDITERRANEAN FOODS.

DISLIKES
PROCESSED FOOD, CUCUMBER, COUSCOUS.

MARGARET LEE TRAINED IN HOTEL MANAGEMENT AT THE LONDON HOTEL SCHOOL, NOW PART OF WESTMINSTER UNIVERSITY. AFTER A LIFETIME OF DOMESTIC COOKING, MARGARET ESTIMATES SHE HAS COOKED OVER 6000 CAKES!

LIKES
ALL PUDS, ROAST BEEF, FISH (DOVER SOLE).

DISLIKES
GARLIC, ONIONS, TRIPE.

ROGER AINGER IS THE UK REPRESENTATIVE FOR VAIL RESORTS. HE HAS RECENTLY TAKEN UP GOLF AND COOKING – CURRIES AND PIES MAINLY. TESTING THESE RECIPES HAS BEEN HIS FIRST EVER BAKING EXPERIENCE.

LIKES
CAMPARI, CHOCOLATE, POPPADUMS.

DISLIKES
RAW FISH (SUSHI), CABBAGE, BURGERS.

MANDY FISHER IS THE ONLY FEMALE WORKING WITH SIX CAKE-LOVING MEN AT A PRIVATE CHARTERED QUANTITY AND BUILDING SURVEYING FIRM. THEY HAVE ENJOYED TESTING HER CAKES AND BAKES THROUGH THE YEARS. SHE ALSO REALLY ENJOYS TRYING OUT NEW DESSERTS AT HOME.

LIKES
MUSSELS, CINNAMON.

DISLIKES
OFFAL, OLIVES, ARTICHOKES.

SIMON EBBS DOES A LOT OF OUTSIDE WORK RESTORING ANCIENT BUILDINGS AND SO REALLY ENJOYS HIS FOOD WHEN HE GET HOME TO HIS COTTAGE IN RUTLAND. HE DOES MOST OF THE COOKING AS HIS PARTNER MANAGED TO BREAK A RANGE COOKER!

LIKES
CHEESE, DARK CHOCOLATE, BLACK PUDDING.

DISLIKES
WEAK COFFEE, HAZELNUTS, SKIMMED MILK.

JACQUI MELVILLE IS A FOOD PHOTOGRAPHER AND IS GAINING CONFIDENCE WITH HER BAKING, AFTER NUMEROUS MISHAPS. **SUZANNE QUINTNER (MUM)** OWNS A SMALL MOROCCAN CONDIMENT BUSINESS IN BRISBANE, AUSTRALIA. SHE IS ALWAYS BAKING FOR HER FAMILY AND FRIENDS.

LIKES
JACQUI: OYSTERS, CHILLI SAUCE, BEEF CARPACCIO.
SUZANNE: SMOKED SALMON, TRADITIONAL JEWISH FOOD.

DISLIKES
JACQUI: CHOCOLATE, CANNED MEAT, MASS PRODUCE FOOD.
SUZANNE: RAW ONION, SALAD LEAVES, CUCUMBER.

THE ROBINSON FAMILY ARE AN ACTIVE FAMILY WHO ARE PASSIONATE ABOUT SKIING AND RUGBY. THEY LOVE TO EXPLORE AND DISCOVER NEW PLACES, ENTERTAIN, AND CAN DANCE AND PARTY WITH THE BEST OF THEM!

LIKES
ANYTHING BARBEQUED, CHILLIES, FRESH FISH.

DISLIKES
TINNED FRUIT, CREAMY SAUCES, FAST FOOD.

COLIN MEEKCOMS' HEART LIVES IN THE ALPS AND HE LOVES TO SPEND AS MUCH TIME AS POSSIBLE SKIING AND BEING IN THE MOUNTAINS. HE HAS WORKED MANY SKI SEASONS BUT IS A NOVICE TO BAKING.

LIKES
OYSTERS, STEAK AND KIDNEY PUD, ALL STINKY CHEESE.

DISLIKES
BEETROOT, BEETROOT, BEETROOT (BEETS)!

ALANDA WHITEHEAD HAS BEEN COOKING FOR AS ALONG AS SHE CAN REMEMBER AND PARTICULARLY ADORES WHEN THE FAMILY CAN ALL SIT DOWN AROUND THE KITCHEN TABLE.

LIKES
LUCY'S FLAPJACKS; TREACLE TART; A ROAST LAMB DINNER.

DISLIKES
TRIPE; PICKLED ONIONS; OYSTERS.

SARITA KATTOJU ENJOYS COOKING AND BAKING TOGETHER. SARITA IS A BUSY WORKING MUM WITH A HECTIC SCHEDULE. SHE LOVES FOOD THAT IS QUICK AND EASY TO MAKE. **ROHIT PABLA (SON)** JOINS IN WITH THE COOKING AND IS PRETTY SELF SUFFICIENT.

LIKES
SARITA AND ROHIT: SEAFOOD PAELLA, CRÈME CARAMEL, CROISSANTS.

DISLIKES
SARITA AND ROHIT: READY MEALS, SALMON CAVIAR AND MELON.

JILL PEREIRA LIVES IN A VILLAGE WHERE THERE SEEMS TO BE A CONSTANT NEED FOR CAKES FOR FUNCTIONS OR EVENTS. SHE IS NOW THE MASTER OF THE LEMON DRIZZLE. JILL IS ALWAYS ON THE LOOK OUT FOR NEW AND INTERESTING (EASY!!) RECIPES.

LIKES
CRUSTY BREAD, ITALIAN FOOD, HOT COFFEE.

DISLIKES
OCTOPUS, TRIPE, SEMOLINA PUDDING.

LYNSEY JONES HAS SPENT 10 WINTERS WORKING IN THE FRENCH ALPS, MOST RECENTLY AS RESORT MANAGER. THIS SUMMER IS RUNNING A CHALET FOR MOUNTAIN BIKERS. HER GUEST HAVE BEEN ENJOYING THE CAKES SHE HAS BEEN TESTING FOR THIS BOOK!

LIKES
SOY SAUCE, ONION, PIMENT DE CAYENNE.

DISLIKES
PINEAPPLE, CELERY, BAKED BEANS.

JANE BOLTON LOVES BAKING AND HAD GREAT FUN TRYING THESE RECIPES IN THE KITCHEN WITH THE KIDS.

LIKES
CHAMPAGNE, CHOCOLATES, KING PRAWNS IN GARLIC.

DISLIKES
CHEESE, PEPPERS, CAULIFLOWER.

A CLASSIC SPONGE CAKE HAS A FEW GOLDEN RULES
WHICH ARE OUTLINED IN THE STEP-BY-STEP GUIDE ON PAGE 42
BUT NOT ALL CAKES ARE MADE THIS WAY – FAR FROM IT.
HAVING HAD THE CHANCE TO DESIGN RECIPES AND MENUS FOR SKI
CHALETS IN DIFFERENT EUROPEAN COUNTRIES AND NORTH AMERICA,
I HAVE GATHERED TIPS, TRICKS AND OUTLANDISH METHODOLOGY
FROM DIFFERENT CORNERS OF THE CAKE WORLD. SOME ARE SO
QUICK TO GET IN THE OVEN IT IS ASTONISHING, AND ONE OR TWO
HAVE LISTS OF INGREDIENTS THAT YOU WOULD NOT BELIEVE
COULD MAKE A CAKE – SO KEEP AN OPEN MIND!

BEFORE YOU PUT ON YOUR APRON SEE PAGE 8 FOR
SOME HELPFUL NOTES.

ONE MORE THING – GOT A FAN OVEN? DON'T FORGET
YOU NEED TO REDUCE THE TEMPERATURE – CONVERSION
CHARTS ARE SHOWN ON PAGE 9.

HAPPY BAKING AND LOTS OF CAKE LOVE!

CAKES

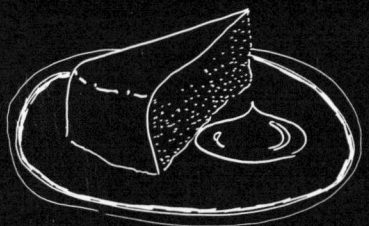

Spiced Honey Cake

PREPARATION	COOKING	MAKES	VEGETARIAN	NUT-FREE
10 mins	1–1½ hours	1 x 500 g (1 lb) loaf (8 slices)		

Pain d'épices in France is a firm, sweet, dryish treat somewhere between a bread and a cake. It is the perfect snack for hiking, picnicking and popping into your pocket for walking the dog. More cake than bread perhaps, but the flavours are wonderful and I adore it. This is my version which is a bit sweeter, a little softer, but still better after a few days in your cake tin so make ahead.

75 g (2½ oz) butter
150 g (5 oz/scant ½ cup) clear honey
75 g (2½ oz/⅓ cup) caster (superfine) sugar
75 g (2½ oz) water
1 egg
175 g (6 oz/scant 1½ cups) plain (all-purpose) flour
5 g (¼ oz) bicarbonate of soda (baking soda)
15 g (½ oz) ground ginger
10 g (⅓ oz) ground cinnamon
pinch of ground nutmeg

1. Preheat the oven to 160°C (320°F/Gas 3). Line a 500 g (1 lb) loaf tin with baking paper.
2. Put the butter, honey, sugar and water in a bowl and microwave for 2 minutes on full power, then stir well.
3. Add the rest of the ingredients and mix with a hand whisk.
4. Turn into the lined loaf tin and bake for 1–1½ hours, until risen and springy to the touch, or until a cocktail stick inserted in the centre comes out clean.
5. Leave to cool in the tin but cover the top with a clean tea (dish) towel as this will help its texture when cool. Wrap well in cling film (plastic wrap) and store in an airtight container.

WHAT THE TESTERS SAY

SAMUEL RAFTER – 'This is quite spicy but I loved it with my espresso.'

STELLA CAUDWELL – 'I loved it! Great with a cuppa.'

BEN COLEBY – 'As a novice I followed this recipe to the letter and it worked. This is a great cake for a pocket on a long walk.'

TIP
YOU CAN ALTER THE LEVELS OF SPICE TO SUIT YOUR TASTES SO MAKE ONCE, WRITE A NOTE ON THE PAGE AND THEN ALTER THE NEXT TIME ROUND.

TIP
ROSE WATER IS AVAILABLE FROM ALL GOOD SUPERMARKETS.

ROSE AND POPPY SEED CAKE

PREPARATION 15 mins | **COOKING** 30 mins | **MAKES** 1 x 23 cm (9 in) cake (10–12 slices) | **VEGETARIAN** | **NUT-FREE**

I lived in France for many years and came across a 'learn English' book that described an English afternoon tea. It was cake, tea and sandwiches but it was presented in a cottage garden surrounded by climbing roses. I lived in the mountains so the only way to try and recreate this idyll for some neighbours who came for tea was to add the rose to my cake! I have since sourced some wonderful edible rose petals on the internet and scatter my cake with these.

FOR THE CAKE

4 eggs
caster (superfine) sugar
self-raising flour
butter and margarine, at room temperature
pinch of salt
50 g (2 oz) poppy seeds
20 g (¾ oz) rose water

FOR THE ROSE BUTTERCREAM

75 g (2½ oz) white chocolate
300 g (10½ oz/2½ cups) icing (confectioners') sugar, sifted
200 g (7 oz) butter, at room temperature
a few drops of pink food colouring
15 g (½ oz) rose water
edible rose petals to scatter over (optional)

1. Preheat the oven to 180°C (350°F/Gas 4). Line a 23 cm (9 in) deep cake tin with baking paper.
2. Weigh the eggs in their shells and then weigh the same amount of sugar, flour, and half the weight in butter and half in margarine.
3. Beat the butter and margarine together with the sugar in a bowl using a wooden spoon or electric whisk. Beat in 1 egg at a time.
4. Sift the flour and salt over, then sprinkle in the poppy seeds and rosewater. Gently fold in with a metal spoon.
5. Turn the cake mix out into the prepared tin and bake for 30 minutes until risen, browned and springy to the touch, or a skewer inserted in the centre comes out clean.
6. Turn it out onto a wire rack, remove the paper and leave to cool.
7. Meanwhile make the buttercream. Melt the chocolate in a bowl over a pan of boiling water then let it cool for at least 10 minutes. This must not be hot when you make the buttercream. Add the icing sugar, butter, colouring and rose water and beat until light and fluffy.
8. Cut the cake in half and sandwich back together with a third of the buttercream. Spread the rest over the top and around the side and scatter with edible rose petals.

WHAT THE TESTERS SAY

JACQUI MELVILLE AND SUNANNE QUINTNER – 'Looked beautiful and the poppy seeds added a really nice crunch. We loved the rose flavour.'

CLAIRE VAN DIJK – 'I love special cakes and this is one. It is simple to make and, if you follow the tips for the perfect sponge, it is light and fluffy. I didn't have rose petals so I bought some freeze-dried raspberries instead. Great flavours.'

ANTONIA ARGENTIER – 'We had no rose petals but we used grated white chocolate instead. I am hooked on poppy seeds and will be adding them to many cake recipes.'

CHOCOLATE AND BEETROOT CAKE

PREPARATION 15 mins | **COOKING** 30 mins | **MAKES** 1 x 20 cm cake (8 in) (8 slices) | **VEGETARIAN** | **NUT-FREE**

If you did not know beetroot (beet) was an ingredient here I think you would struggle to indentify it – why bother adding it then, you ask? Well, it adds a real depth of flavour, an earthiness and sweetness and I think, seems to make it even more chocolatey. I love the vivid pink icing made with the beetroot juice but you can smother it with ganache or chocolate fudge icing if you prefer. Whichever way, this is a wonderfully rich chocolate cake. Remember to weigh the beetroot after you have peeled and grated it!

FOR THE CAKE

250 g (9 oz) dark chocolate
240 g (8 oz) raw, finely grated beetroot (beets)
3 eggs
200 g (7 oz/scant 1 cup) caster (superfine) sugar
150 g (5 oz/1¼ cups) plain (all-purpose) flour
10 g (½ oz) baking powder
pinch of salt
100 g (3½ oz) vegetable oil

FOR THE DECORATION

150 g (5 oz) butter, at room temperature
250 g (9 oz/2 cups) icing (confectioners') sugar, sifted
squeezed juice from the grated beetroot (beets)
50 g (2 oz) dark chocolate

1. Preheat the oven to 190°C (375°F/Gas 5). Line a 20 cm (8 in) round, deep cake tin with baking paper.
2. Break the chocolate into small pieces, place in a bowl and microwave for 1 minute on full power. Remove, stir and repeat every 30 seconds (stirring in between each melt). Alternatively, place the bowl over a pan of simmering water, stirring occasionally until the chocolate is melted.
3. Allow to cool for 5 minutes. This is important!
4. Squeeze the beetroot to remove the excess juice and reserve for the buttercream. Set aside.
5. Add the eggs and sugar to the cooled chocolate and whisk until thick.
6. Add the flour, baking powder, salt, oil and squeezed raw beetroot and fold the mixture together using a metal spoon until blended well.
7. Turn into the prepared cake tin and bake for 30 minutes or until it is springy to the touch or a cocktail stick inserted in the centre comes out clean.
8. Meanwhile make the buttercream by beating the butter, icing sugar and beetroot juice together until smooth, fluffy and vivid pink in colour.
9. Turn the cake out on to a wire rack, remove the paper and leave to cool. Pipe or spread the buttercream over the cake. Make squiggles or the word 'beetroot' using the chocolate (see page 199). When set, arrange on top of the cake.

WHAT THE TESTERS SAY

LYDIA CUFFLIN AND SIMON CHILDS – 'This stays really yummy for a good few days and the beetroot and chocolate are surprisingly good together. Delicious!'

PENNY VICKERS – 'I was amazed that this was so chocolatey and moist. My buttercream was very vivid so I might do a chocolate buttercream next time.'

FIONA GALLAGHER AND OLLIE EVANS – 'We ate this at 5p.m. with coffee and friends for a treat. Easy to make – really good, earthy flavours and I imagine it would be good with clotted cream.'

TIP
WEAR LATEX GLOVES WHEN GRATING THE BEETROOT TO PREVENT PINK FINGERS!

TIP

MAKE SURE YOUR BANANAS ARE REALLY RIPE TO GET THE FULL FLAVOUR AND TEXTURE FOR THIS CAKE.

BANOFFI CUPCAKES

PREPARATION	COOKING	MAKES	VEGETARIAN	NUT-FREE
15 mins	20 mins	10 cupcakes		

These are tooth-curlingly sweet with a cunning caramel centre – but bananas, caramel and chocolate – what's not to like? You can buy condensed milk caramel or you can make it yourself. Simply put a can of sweetened condensed milk unopened in a deep saucepan and cover with water. Put on a lid, bring to the boil, reduce the heat and simmer for one hour. Leave to cool in the pan of water. You can do several cans at once and store them in the cupboard for up to six months.

4 ripe bananas
250 g (9 oz) butter, at room temperature
200 g (7 oz/scant 1 cup) demerara (raw) sugar
2 eggs
225 g (8 oz/1¾ cups) self-raising flour, sifted
397 g (14 oz) can condensed milk caramel
200 g (7 oz/1⅔ cups) icing (confectioners') sugar, sifted
100 g (3½ oz) dark chocolate, grated

1. Preheat the oven to 180°C (350°F/Gas 4). Line a muffin tin with cake cases.
2. Put the bananas in a mixing bowl and mash them with a fork. Add half the butter and sugar and beat well until smoothish. Add the eggs, beat again, then using a metal spoon fold in the flour.
3. Fill the muffin cases half-way up with the mixture.
4. Open the can of caramelised condensed milk and put a teaspoon of the caramel into the centre of each cupcake (reserve a third of the caramel for the topping). Then cover with more mixture so the condensed milk is sealed by cake mix all round. The mixture should now be three-quarters of the way up the cake cases.
5. Bake for 20 minutes or until springy to the touch. Cool on a wire rack.
6. Beat the rest of the caramelised condensed milk, the remaining butter and the icing sugar together to make the topping and pile it or pipe it onto the top of the cakes.
7. Sprinkle with the grated chocolate to decorate.

WHAT THE THE TESTERS SAY

ANNETTE MEEKCOMS – 'These were sweet and sticky and the children ate them all!'

KERRY GREGORY – 'These were rich, but my friends and I polished them off one lunchtime. The banana cake would be great as a stand-alone cake too.'

BEN COLEBY – 'I made this as a 20 cm (8 in) round cake but did not put the caramel into the raw cake mix. I cut it in half when cooked and filled it with the caramel – I did not top with butter cream but it was delicious and sweet even so. I am very new to baking but it worked for me!'

ST CLEMENTS CAKE

PREPARATION
15 mins + 40 mins for oranges & lemons

COOKING
45 mins to 1 hour

MAKES
1 x 20 cm cake (8 slices)

VEGETARIAN

GLUTEN-FREE

'Oranges and lemons say the bells of St Clements'. This delicious cake is made with both lemons and oranges – hence its name. It is so moist that it can be served warm as a pud or cold as a wonderful treat with a good coffee or a cuppa. A dollop of thick cream or crème fraîche is excellent alongside. It keeps well, so make it ahead if you have a special date when you want to serve it. This gorgeous creation is also gluten-free, so is something to be enjoyed by all.

3 large eating oranges
2 lemons
6 eggs
250 g (9 oz/generous 1 cup) caster (superfine) sugar
275 g (10 oz/2⅔ cups) ground almonds
7 g (¼ oz) gluten-free baking powder
icing (confectioners') sugar, for dusting

1 Preheat the oven to 180°C (350°F/Gas 4). Line a 20 cm (8 in) round, deep cake tin with baking paper.
2 Cook the oranges and lemons in a pan of boiling water for 40 minutes, until they are bloated and soft.
3 Remove from the water, cool a little if you need to, then cut in half and remove any pips.
4 Put the whole oranges and lemons (peel, pith and all) into a food processor, or into a bowl and use a hand blender, to whizz the fruit to a smooth pulp.
5 Add the rest of the ingredients. Mix to a thick batter and pour it into the prepared tin.
6 Bake for 45 minutes to 1 hour, until the cake is risen and springy to the touch, or a cocktail stick inserted in the centre comes out clean.
7 Cool slightly in the tin, then turn out, dust with icing sugar and serve warm with thick cream or custard as a pud or allow to cool completely in the tin before turning out, dusting with icing sugar and serving.

WHAT THE TESTERS SAY

MARGARET LEE – 'I used to do something very similar in a pastry case but it's better as a cake. I cooked this for a dinner party for a coeliac friend.'

TOM ROBERTS – 'I loved it and it was so simple to make.'

HELEN WOOLDRIDGE – 'An excellent cake for gluten-free guests in the chalet and it lasts a long time kept in the fridge.'

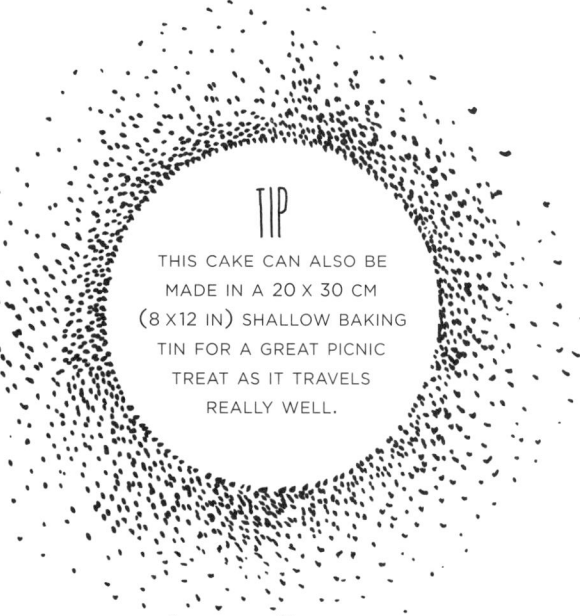

TIP
THIS CAKE CAN ALSO BE MADE IN A 20 X 30 CM (8 X 12 IN) SHALLOW BAKING TIN FOR A GREAT PICNIC TREAT AS IT TRAVELS REALLY WELL.

SWEDISH APPLE CAKE

PREPARATION	COOKING	MAKES	VEGETARIAN	NUT-FREE
15 mins	35–40 mins	1 large tart (10–12 slices)		

I loved my time working in Sweden in the 80s. One of my long lasting memories is apple cake. It was offered in every restaurant, cafe and shop and served as a cake, a pud or a snack. I tried many recipes but this was my favourite and if you make it in a 25 cm (10 in) tin it looks more like a tart than a cake, so is perfect served warm as a wonderful autumn pud with a dollop of thick cream.

6 sharp eating apples
150 g (5 oz) butter
3 eggs, beaten
250 g (9 oz/2 cups) plain (all-purpose) flour
10 g (½ oz) baking powder
7 g (¼ oz) ground cinnamon
150 g (5 oz/⅔ cup) caster (superfine) sugar

FOR THE TOPPING
25 g (1 oz) butter
60 g (2 oz/¼ cup) demerara (raw) sugar
3 g (⅛ oz) ground cinnamon
icing (confectioners') sugar, for dusting

1. Preheat the oven to 180°C (350°F/Gas 4). Line a 25 cm (10 in) flan tin with baking paper.
2. Coarsely grate 3 of the apples with skins on, discarding the cores.
3. Peel, core and slice the remaining 3 apples.
4. Melt the butter in a large saucepan then remove from the heat. Add the grated apples and eggs and mix well. Add the flour, baking powder, cinnamon and sugar, mix until well combined, then turn into the prepared tin.
5. Leaving 2 cm (¾ in) around the edge, arrange the sliced apples on top in a spiral or rows. The edge will form a sort of crust around the edge of this cake.
6. For the topping, melt the butter in a saucepan, stir in the sugar and cinnamon. The mixture will be granular, so sprinkle it over the top of the apples.
7. Bake for 35–40 minutes or until risen and browned. If you want to serve it hot, this can be cooked ahead and reheated at the same temperature for 15 minutes, but otherwise leave it to go cold, dust with icing sugar and serve with a dollop of thick cream.

WHAT THE TESTERS SAY

GEMMA HEDGES – 'My cake tin was smaller so it was a deeper cake and took a bit longer to cook, so I covered the top with foil to stop it burning. This is a really nice cake and would make a good pudding.'

STELLA CAUDWELL – 'Just my sort of cake and I will be doing it again in windfall season!'

JILL PEREIRA – 'A great cake – almost more like a tart than a cake but nothing wrong with that!'

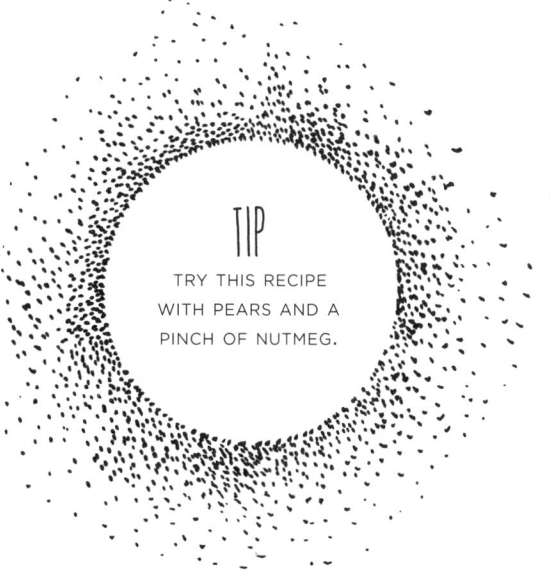

TIP
TRY THIS RECIPE WITH PEARS AND A PINCH OF NUTMEG.

CHOCOLATE SPREAD CAKE

PREPARATION
2 mins

COOKING
25 – 30 mins

MAKES
1 x 20 cm (8 in) cake (8 slices)

VEGETARIAN

I was skiing in North America when I read a recipe for a cake on the back of a chocolate spread jar. I did not make a note of the quantities but remembered the ingredients because they seemed so odd. A few attempts at cooking it and tweaking the amounts resulted in this wondrously instant, fabulously easy, soft and succulent chocolate cake. It is a real hit with those who want to have some fun with young children stirring and baking with little fuss, while the flavour is great and gives a milky sweet chocolate cake which seems popular with so many.

400 g (14 oz) jar chocolate and hazelnut spread, plus extra for topping
3 eggs
125 g (4 oz/1 cup) plain (all-purpose) flour
10 g (½ oz) baking powder
200 g (7 oz) cream cheese
Nut Brittle (see page 85), or use shop-bought, crushed (optional)

1. Preheat the oven to 180°C (350°F/Gas 4). Line a 20 cm (8 in) deep cake tin with baking paper.
2. Mix everything together in a bowl with a whisk or spoon then turn into the prepared tin.
3. Bake for 25-30 minutes or until springy to the touch.
4. Turn out onto a wire rack, remove the baking paper and leave to cool.
5. Top with more chocolate spread and scatter crushed nut brittle over, if using.

WHAT THE TESTERS SAY

JACK MEEKCOMS – 'I made this all on my own and ate nearly all of it myself too – great cake!'

MICHAEL CUFFLIN – 'We love it. I cover it with more chocolate spread.'

MIA AND HARRY ROGERS – 'We loved it, so we baked a big one and covered it with chocolate spread frosting. Delicious.'

TIP
FOR A MORE ELABORATE FINISH, YOU COULD FILL AND TOP IT WITH SAM'S FUDGE ICING (SEE PAGE 195), A RICH GANACHE OR CHOCOLATE SPREAD FROSTING (SEE PAGE 194).

TIP
I ADD MORE GINGER THAN IT SAYS BUT TRY THIS FIRST AND THEN GO FOR IT! YOU CAN ALSO MAKE THIS IN A 20 CM (8 IN) CAKE TIN

DARK GINGER CAKE

PREPARATION	COOKING	MAKES	VEGETARIAN	NUT-FREE
10 mins	1 hour	1 x 20 cm (8 in) round cake or 1 x 1 kg (2 lb) loaf (8–10 slices)		

I would walk a long way for good ginger cake and for that reason I have cooked many. When we were small we would make fairy cakes at my Grandmother's house using her old Bero cooking booklet. I came across this wondrous little cookbook amongst some other papers many years after she died and looking through it, saw a simple recipe for ginger cake. A few tweaks later, the addition of a bit of microwave melting and here it is – a delicious, sticky, dark and gingery cake. It is better after a few days, so make it ahead if you have a special occasion. Bake on, ginger lovers!

80 g (3 oz) butter
80 g (3 oz) black treacle (molasses)
150 g (3 oz) golden (corn) syrup
125 g (4 oz/generous ½ cup) caster (superfine) sugar
225 g (8 oz/1¾ cups) self-raising flour
20 g (¾ oz) ground ginger
5 g (¼ oz) ground cinnamon
250 g (9 oz) milk
1 egg
thick white icing and chopped crystallised ginger, for topping (optional)

1. Preheat the oven to 160°C (320°F/Gas 3). Line a 1 kg (2 lb) loaf tin with baking paper.
2. In a bowl put the butter, treacle, syrup and caster sugar and microwave on full power for 2 minutes. Stir well.
3. Beat in the remaining ingredients and turn into the prepared tin.
4. Put in the oven and bake for 1 hour or until risen and springy to the touch.
5. Leave to cool for 15 minutes in the tin then remove and wrap in double cling film (plastic wrap), while still warm – this will help it get stickier as it cools.
6. Top with thick white icing and chopped crystallised ginger when cold.

WHAT THE TESTERS SAY

BRENDAN CROFT – 'This is a real winner – I cannot fault it except that I would add even more ginger for me.'

SARA MCDONALD – 'Still fantastic and seems even stickier after 5 days – a great cake to keep in the tin.'

MARGARET LEE – 'Easy and quickly done – it would make a nice pudding with crème anglaise.'

PERFECT VICTORIA SANDWICH CAKE

PREPARATION	COOKING	MAKES	VEGETARIAN	NUT-FREE
15 mins	20–25 mins	1 x 20 cm (8 in) sponge cake (8 slices)		

Queen Victoria's preferred afternoon tea cake was a plain sponge sandwiched with raspberry jam and dusted with caster sugar – known to us as a Victoria sandwich. If you felt like adding a touch of whipped cream or buttercream to the filling it would no longer be a Victoria sandwich according to the Women's Institute, and if you entered one of their cake competitions with such additions you would be immediately disqualified. If you are not entering such a competition then you are free to fill it with whatever you like – the choice is yours.

4 eggs
caster (superfine) sugar
self-raising flour
butter and margarine, at room temperature
pinch of salt
10 g (½ oz) water
good-quality jam (or make your own, see page 192)
vanilla buttercream (see page 196) or fresh whipped cream (optional)
caster (superfine) or icing (confectioners') sugar, to serve

1. Preheat the oven to 180°C (350°F/Gas 4). Line two 20 cm (8 in) sandwich tins.
2. Weigh the 4 eggs in their shells and weigh out the same amount of sugar and flour and half their weight each of butter and margarine (or all butter, but you get a lighter mix with a combination of the two).
3. Beat the butter and margarine together with the sugar in a mixing bowl with a wooden spoon or an electric whisk until pale, smooth and fluffy, about 3 minutes. Do not over-beat as this can make the cake sink later.
4. Beat in 1 egg at a time, mixing well after each addition until soft and fluffy again.
5. Sift the flour and salt over and gently fold in using a metal spoon (do not over-mix or you will knock all the air out). It will be slightly too thick, so add the water and fold in gently.
6. Divide the mixture between the 2 tins and level the surface with the back of a spoon or a palette knife.
7. Bake for 20–25 minutes, until the cakes have risen and are springy to the touch, or when a cocktail stick inserted in the centre comes out clean.
8. Turn the cakes out onto a wire rack so they can cool with air around them, which will help make them lighter.
9. When they are completely cool, sandwich together with good jam and whipped cream or buttercream, if liked, and dust with caster or icing sugar to serve.

WHAT THE TESTERS SAY

LYNSEY JONES AND HELEN WOOLDRIDGE – 'A perfect cake – I kept it simple and added fresh strawberries. My tin was a bit big so not quite as tall as I wanted, so check tin sizes or make extra cake mixture'

ROGER AINGER – 'Went for the heart attack option and filled it with jam and cream! Absolute baking beginner and making a Victoria sponge felt like real baking. I am looking forward to trying it again to achieve perfection.'

FIONA GALLAGHER AND OLLIE EVANS – 'We added whipped cream flavoured with a dash of vanilla extract and piled it high with fruit.'

TIP
THERE ARE SOME GOLDEN RULES TO MAKING A GREAT SPONGE ON PAGES 42-3, SO READ THEM FIRST.

VICTORIA SPONGE STEP-BY-STEP

1. LINE YOUR CAKE TINS IN ONE OF THREE WAYS: (1) USE CAKE TIN LINERS; (2) CUT OUT A CIRCLE OF BAKING PAPER LARGE ENOUGH TO LINE THE TIN COMPLETELY, THEN CUT INCISIONS ROUND THE EDGES; (3) GREASE THE TINS WITH THE BUTTER PAPER OR OIL AND LINE THE BASES WITH A DISC OF BAKING PAPER.

2. USING AN ELECTRIC HAND WHISK OR A WOODEN SPOON, BEAT THE SOFTENED FAT (I USE HALF BUTTER AND HALF MARGARINE) WITH THE SUGAR IN A MIXING BOWL FOR ABOUT 3 MINUTES UNTIL PALE, SMOOTH AND FLUFFY.

3. ADD THE EGGS ONE AT A TIME, BEATING WELL AFTER EACH ADDITION UNTIL YOU HAVE A MIXTURE THAT IS A SOFTER VERSION OF WHAT IT LOOKED LIKE BEFORE YOU ADDED THE EGG.

4. SIFT THE FLOUR AND SALT OVER THE MIXTURE. THIS WILL ADD MORE AIR TO THE CAKE AND MAKE SURE THERE ARE NO LUMPS IN THE FLOUR, SO WILL GIVE A GOOD LIGHT, EVEN TEXTURE.

5. USE A METAL SPOON TO GENTLY FOLD THE MIXTURE OVER AND OVER UNTIL COMBINED. DON'T OVER-MIX OR YOU WILL KNOCK OUT ALL THE AIR.

6. ADD THE MEASURED AMOUNT OF WATER TO LOOSEN THE CAKE MIX AND HELP GIVE A LIGHT SPONGE AND GENTLY FOLD THIS INTO THE MIXTURE WITH THE METAL SPOON.

7 SPOON THE MIXTURE INTO THE TIN OR DIVIDE IT EQUALLY BETWEEN 2 PREPARED SANDWICH TINS. SPREAD IT TO AN EVEN LAYER WITH THE BACK OF THE SPOON. BAKE IMMEDIATELY IN A PREHEATED OVEN AT 180°C (350°F/GAS 4).

8 PLACE THE CAKE AND TIN ONTO A WIRE RACK. TO TEST THE CAKES ARE DONE INSERT A COCKTAIL STICK OR SKEWER INTO THE CENTRE. IT SHOULD COME OUT CLEAN. ALTERNATIVELY, THE CAKE SHOULD SPRING BACK IF LIGHTLY PRESSED WITH YOUR FINGER.

9 THE SIMPLEST WAY TO REMOVE YOUR CAKE FROM THE TIN IS TO PLACE ANOTHER WIRE RACK ON THE TOP OF YOUR CAKE, BEING CAREFUL NOT TO BURN YOURSELF. LEAVE THE CAKE TO COOL SLIGHTLY.

10 CAREFULLY FLIP THE CAKE AROUND, HOLDING ON TO THE EDGES OF THE WIRE RACKS AS YOU DO SO. THE CAKE SHOULD NOW BE UPSIDE DOWN. LIFT OFF THE TOP WIRE RACK.

11 REMOVE THE CAKE TIN AND PAPER AND LEAVE TO COOL COMPLETELY. IF MAKING ONE DEEP CAKE, SLICE IT IN HALF HORIZONTALLY, USING A CAKE LEVELLER OR CUTTING TOWARDS THE CENTRE ALL ROUND WITH A SHARP BREAD KNIFE.

12 SPREAD JAM OR YOUR CHOSEN FILLING OVER ONE SPONGE. CAREFULLY SLIDE THE SECOND SPONGE OVER THE JAM. DUST THE TOP WITH CASTER (SUPERFINE) SUGAR OR SIFTED ICING (CONFECTIONERS') SUGAR.

TIP

I ALWAYS KEEP A STOCK OF STALE CRUMBS IN THE FREEZER – THEY ARE USEFUL FOR SO MANY THINGS, NOT JUST THIS LOVELY CAKE.

ITALIAN CITRUS AND ALMOND CAKE

PREPARATION	COOKING	MAKES	VEGETARIAN	DAIRY-FREE
5 mins	40–50 mins	1 x 20 cm (8 in) cake (8 slices)		

The other Lucy loves Italy and a lot of her recipes wend their way back to the UK with her after a visit. This syrupy-sweet little something is best enjoyed sitting down with a really good cup of coffee or a glass of sticky liqueur – why not? What time of day you enjoy it is up to you. It is a great pud for lunch or dinner, served with cream, but is just as delightful mid morning or as part of a decadent afternoon tea. The bay-flavoured syrup is truly unusual but adds an exotic flavour to this cake.

FOR THE CAKE

200 g (7 oz/generous ¾ cup) caster (superfine) sugar
200 g (7 oz) sunflower or olive oil
4 eggs
50 g (2 oz) stale (but not dry) breadcrumbs
100 g (3½ oz/1 cup) ground almonds
5 g (¼ oz) baking powder
finely grated zest of 1 orange and 1 lemon

FOR THE SYRUP

juice of the orange and lemon
100 g (3½ oz/scant ½ cup) granulated sugar
2 bay leaves

1. Preheat the oven to 180°C (350°F/Gas 4). Line a 20 cm (8 in) deep cake tin with baking paper.
2. Whisk together the sugar, oil and eggs until pale and frothy, preferably using an electric hand whisk.
3. Add the breadcrumbs, almonds, baking powder and zests and fold into the egg mixture using a metal spoon.
4. Turn the mixture into the tin and cook for 40–50 minutes, or until a cocktail stick inserted in the centre comes out clean. Leave to cool in the tin while you make the syrup.
5. Put the fruit juices, sugar and bay leaves in a small saucepan and heat gently, without boiling, until all the sugar is dissolved. Then bring to the boil and simmer for 2 minutes.
6. While still warm, carefully turn the cake out, remove the baking paper and place on a serving plate. Prick it all over (use a skewer or cocktail stick) and pour on the syrup a little at a time until the whole cake is well soaked – this should pretty much use all the syrup. It will keep well covered with cling film (plastic wrap) and stored in the fridge but it does not freeze well.

WHAT THE TESTERS SAY

NAOMI AND RUTH HULME – 'This coffee-time treat to share with friends has a different sort of texture to usual cakes but is still good.'

MARGARET LEE – 'My husband loves all things citrus and this no exception – we had it for pudding with whipped cream.'

LYNSEY JONES AND HELEN WOOLDRIDGE – 'This has no flour (just breadcrumbs) so has a much denser texture than afternoon tea cake. However, it is perfect as a pud or something to eat with coffee – full of flavour and an unusual treat.'

SAM'S EASY CHOCOLATE FUDGE CAKE

PREPARATION	COOKING	MAKES	VEGETARIAN	NUT-FREE
5 mins	45 mins	1 x 20 cm (8 in) cake (8 slices)		

My son Sam has baked since he was small, and for him, nothing comes close to a chocolate fudge cake. Because of that he has made many and this is his perfected cake with his own fudge icing – bravo Sam, we love this one! For extra decadence, top with ganache icing, but brush the cooled cake first with melted apricot jam so that the icing does not break the cake.

60 g (2 oz/½ cup) cocoa powder
300 g (10½ oz/1⅓ cups) caster (superfine) sugar
250 g (9 oz) boiling water
125 g (4 oz) butter, at room temperature
225 g (8 oz/1⅔ cups) self-raising flour
5 g (¼ oz) bicarbonate of soda (baking soda) or baking powder
5 g (¼ oz) vanilla extract
2 eggs

SAM'S CHOCOLATE FUDGE ICING
100 g (3½ oz) butter
60 g (2 oz/½ cup) cocoa powder, plus extra to decorate
250 g (9 oz/2 cups) icing (confectioners') sugar, sifted
water, to thin

1. Preheat the oven to 180°C (350°F/Gas 4). Line a 20 cm (8 in) deep cake tin with baking paper.
2. Put the cocoa, sugar and boiling water into a mixing bowl and whisk with an electric hand whisk until smooth.
3. Add the rest of the ingredients and beat with the whisk until smooth.
4. This will be a batter mixture in texture. Pour into the prepared tin.
5. Bake for 45 minutes or until springy to the touch or when a cocktail stick inserted in the centre comes out clean.
6. Turn out onto a wire rack, remove the paper and leave to cool.
7. To make the icing, melt the butter and cocoa in a saucepan then add the icing sugar and just enough water to loosen the icing so it is really thick and spreadable (you may need several spoonfuls of water). Pile it on the top of the cake and spread over the top and sides so there is a really thick layer all over. Leave to set. Decorate with white chocolate buttons or dust cocoa powder before serving.

WHAT THE TESTERS SAY

KAJAL MISTRY – 'Soooo easy to make and absolutely delicious! There's no need for the icing if you find it too chocolatey. Simply serve warm with fresh cream or a scoop of vanilla ice cream.'

BRENDAN CROFT – 'It smelt amazing when cooking and the icing was thick and fantastic. I served it to friends for a birthday party with ice cream and fizzy Champagne.'

GEMMA HEDGES – 'You could top it with raspberries and serve it with chocolate sauce for a pud – it's easy and delicious, I can't say more.'

TIP
TOP WITH CHOCOLATE BUTTONS WHILE THE FUDGE ICING IS STILL WARM AND THEY WILL 'MELT' INTO PLACE!

TIP
THIS CAKE IS MOIST AND GORGEOUS WITHOUT THE NEED FOR A STICKY TOPPING, MAKING IT THE PERFECT PICNIC CAKE.

APPLE AND RYE CAKE

PREPARATION
15 mins

COOKING
30–35 mins

MAKES
1 x 500 g (1 lb) loaf (8 slices)

VEGETARIAN

Creating cake recipes for chalet guests is not just about simplicity, it is also about highlighting local ingredients so that they get a real flavour of where they are staying. This cake was created to embrace a local rye flour from the Tyrol and the rye does give it a great texture. It is better after a few days so, when possible, make it in advance and store in an airtight container.

75 g (2½ oz) butter
150 g (5 oz/scant ¾ cup) demerara (raw) sugar
75 g (2½ oz) milk
2 apples, washed and coarsely grated, including the skin
1 egg
8 g (⅓ oz) ground cinnamon
150 g (5 oz/1½ cups) rye flour
50 g (2 oz/scant ½ cup) ground almonds
10 g (½ oz) baking powder
25 g (1 oz/¼ cup) flaked almonds, to decorate

1. Preheat the oven to 180°C (350°F/Gas 4). Line a 500 g (1 lb) loaf tin with baking paper.
2. Put the butter, sugar and milk into a saucepan and warm until the sugar has dissolved and the butter has melted. Remove from the heat and cool for a few minutes.
3. Add the grated apple, egg, cinnamon, flour, ground almonds and baking powder. Mix well.
4. Transfer to the prepared tin. Sprinkle on top with the flaked almonds.
5. Bake for 30–35 minutes until browned and the centre springs back when pressed gently or when a cocktail stick inserted into the centre of the cake comes out clean.
6. Leave to cool in the tin, then turn out, remove the baking paper and store in an airtight container.

WHAT THE TESTERS SAY

HATTIE CUFFLIN – 'I had never used rye flour before and would have thought the cake might be doughy and heavy but it was light and moist and lovely. I would add more cinnamon as I love it!'

SIMON EBBS – 'This was a great result for me as I do breads but not so many cakes. I took slices of it to work – a real treat.'

IAN MEEKCOMS – 'I like cakes that are not too sweet and this fits the bill – a great cake for me.'

WEIRD AND WONDERFUL BANANA CAKE

PREPARATION
5 mins

COOKING
45–55 mins

MAKES
1 x 1 kg (2 lb) loaf or 20 cm (8 in) round cake (8 slices)

VEGETARIAN

NUT-FREE

Brace yourselves – this cake is made with mayonnaise! But mayonnaise is made from eggs and oil so actually, not so weird? It is one of Lucy LT's 'wonder cakes'. She has been baking this for years and serving it cold as a cake, or warm with thick cream and thick toffee sauce as a pudding – oh yes! I don't like bananas, so created the carrot and parsnip versions. We've used Hellmann's mayonnaise as it has around 8 per cent egg content. Some other brands have less and, as in any cake recipe, the proportion of egg is important, so add a little extra mayo if it has less egg.

250 g (9 oz) very ripe bananas (about 3, peeled weight)
200 g (7 oz/1 cup) soft light brown sugar
250 g (9 oz/1 cup) mayonnaise
100 g (3½ oz) water or strong coffee
250 g (9 oz/2 cups) plain (all-purpose) flour
10 g (½ oz) bicarbonate of soda (baking soda)
pinch of salt
demerara (raw) sugar, for sprinkling

1. Preheat the oven to 180°C (350°F/Gas 4). Line a 1 kg (2 lb) loaf tin with baking paper.
2. Mash the bananas to a smooth paste.
3. Add the sugar with the mayo, mix well with a wooden spoon and add the water or coffee.
4. Add in the dry ingredients and mix well.
5. Pour into the prepared tin and sprinkle with demerara. Bake for 45–55 minutes until risen and firm to the touch. Turn out onto a wire rack, remove the paper and leave to cool.
6. Store in a cool place in an airtight container or well wrapped in cling film (plastic wrap) and foil. It will stay beautifully moist for 4–5 days.

VARIATIONS

CARROT CAKE

As the banana cake, but replace the bananas with 250 g (9 oz) coarsely grated carrot and add 3 g (⅛ oz) each of ground ginger and cinnamon, a pinch of ground nutmeg and the finely grated zest of 1 orange. Bake in a 20 cm (8 in) round, deep cake tin, lined with baking paper. When baked and cooled, top with cream cheese frosting (see page 197), adding the finely grated zest of 1 orange.

PARSNIP CAKE

As the banana cake, but replace the bananas with 250 g (9 oz) coarsely grated parsnips and add 7 g (¼ oz) ground ginger. Bake in a 20 cm (8 in) round, deep cake tine, lined with baking paper. When baked and cooled, top with thick white icing and sprinkle with chopped crystallised ginger.

WHAT THE TESTERS SAY

GEMMA HEDGES – 'I made this as the carrot cake – it was light and scrummy, not dense like many carrot cakes. A brilliant recipe.'

JENNY GREENWOOD – 'Very easy to make. I was shocked by the mayonnaise but it turned out perfectly. I would make this again.'

MARK SCILLEY – 'I made the banana cake as a round cake and I was so proud of my first baking attempt ever that I shared it with all my work colleagues.'

Opposite: left, Carrot Cake; right, Mini Banana Loaves

TIP

FOR EXTRA LOVELINESS ADD SOME CRUMBLED HONEYCOMB, THE SEEDS OF 6-8 CARDAMOM PODS, ROUGHLY CHOPPED PECANS OR WALNUTS AND CHOCOLATE CHIPS, OR DRAINED STEM GINGER, FINELY CHOPPED.

TIP
ENHANCE THE FLAVOUR OF THE WALNUTS BY TOASTING THEM FOR 5 MINUTES IN THE OVEN BEFORE GRINDING.

GREEK COFFEE AND WALNUT CAKE

PREPARATION	COOKING	MAKES	VEGETARIAN
10 mins	30–40 mins	1 x 20 cm (8 in) cake (8 slices)	

I ate something like this on the Greek island of Ithaca and came across it again in a Mediterranean deli in London. Following the advice of the shopkeeper, and using home ingredients, this is my version of the original Greek treat I enjoyed so much. It is for coffee lovers everywhere. Serve warm as a pudding with a dollop of Greek yoghurt or cold for afternoon tea.

FOR THE CAKE

150 g (5 oz/1¼ cups) walnuts (see tip, opposite)
175 g (6 oz) butter, at room temperature
175 g (6 oz/¾ cup) caster (superfine) sugar
3 g (⅛ oz) ground cinnamon
2 eggs
175 g (6 oz) plain yoghurt
175 g (6 oz/1⅓ cups) self-raising flour, sifted
icing (confectioners') sugar, to dust

FOR THE SYRUP

500 ml (1 lb 2 oz) water
15 g (½ oz) instant coffee granules
300 g (10½ oz/1⅓ cups) caster (superfine) sugar

1. Preheat the oven to 170°C (325°F/Gas 3½). Line a 20 cm (8 in) round, deep cake tin with baking paper.
2. Toast the nuts for 5 minutes on a baking sheet. Cool. Chop 25 g (1 oz/¼ cup) and put the rest in a container. Using a hand blender blitz them until coarsely ground.
3. Put the butter, sugar, ground nuts, cinnamon, eggs and yoghurt into a bowl and mix until combined.
4. Add the flour and chopped walnuts and fold the mixture together with a metal spoon.
5. Turn the mixture into the prepared cake tin and bake for 30–40 minutes, until it is springy to the touch or a cocktail stick inserted in the centre comes out clean.
6. Meanwhile make the syrup. Put the ingredients into a saucepan, heat gently until the sugar dissolves then boil rapidly with no lid until it has reduced to 200 ml (7 fl oz/¾ cup) – measure it.
7. Remove the cake from the oven and, while it is still warm spoon half of the coffee syrup all over the top. Let it cool completely then remove from the tin, peel off the baking paper and dust the top with icing sugar. Then serve with the rest of the syrup in a jug. For an extra indulgence, serve with a dollop of fresh yoghurt.

WHAT THE TESTERS SAY

LYNSEY JONES AND HELEN WOOLDRIDGE – 'We added icing and some crushed coffee beans on the top – one chalet guest announced that it was amazing and wonderful.'

MARGARET LEE – 'I gave it to one of the lovely girls who come and clean for us who is a good cook – she said it was the best cake she'd had in absolutely ages.'

DI PALUMBO – 'This cake is fantastic – it is really grown-up in flavour and texture. Served warm it makes a fabulous pudding piled high with fresh Greek yoghurt.'

BOMBAY BUTTERFLY CAKES

PREPARATION 15 mins | **COOKING** 15–20 mins | **MAKES** 12 | **VEGETARIAN** | **NUT-FREE**

Looking for something a little different? Look no further. These cakes happened by accident – the other Lucy and I were making cakes with elderflower syrup and wanted them to be slightly more yellow but alas we had no yellow food colouring. Opening the drawer we both saw the turmeric at the same time. Twenty minutes later the cakes were most certainly yellow and what a fabulous flavour! A few experiments with spices and floral flavours and we had our Bombay butterfly cake recipe.

FOR THE CAKES
4 eggs
caster (superfine) sugar
butter and/or margarine, at room temperature
self-raising flour
pinch of salt
5 g (¼ oz) ground ginger
50 g (2 oz) crystallised ginger, chopped
10 g (½ oz) water
lemon grass and ginger cordial, to drizzle

FOR THE BUTTERCREAM
150 g (5 oz) butter
pinch of ground turmeric
250 g (9 oz/2 cups) icing (confectioners') sugar
15 g (½ oz) lemon grass and ginger cordial
crystallised ginger, cut in slivers, to decorate

1. Preheat the oven to 190°C (375°F/Gas 5) and line the muffin tin with cake cases.
2. Weigh the eggs and measure the same weight of sugar, butter and self-raising flour.
3. Whisk the butter and sugar together (follow the tips on page 42–43 for the perfect sponge).
4. Add the eggs one at a time and then sift in the flour, salt and ground ginger. Fold the ingredients together adding the chopped crystallised ginger. Spoon into the muffin tins so they are three-quarters full.
5. Bake for 15–20 minutes or until risen and springy to the touch. While they are still hot, douse with a good slug of ginger and lemon grass cordial. Leave to cool completely.
6. Make the buttercream by beating the ingredients together in a bowl.
7. Take a small serrated knife and, holding it at an angle tip towards the centre, cut around so you remove a conical-shaped piece of cake that goes to a deep point at the centre.
8. Pipe or pile the buttercream into the hole and then cut the removed cake in half and place it back on top like butterfly wings. Decorate with an extra piece of crystallised ginger.

VARIATIONS

ROSE AND CHILLI – add a hefty pinch of chilli flakes to the cake mix, omitting the ginger and add 10 g (½ oz) rose water. Add a few drops of pink colouring to the cake mix. Drizzle the hot cakes with rosehip syrup and make the buttercream with rose water, pinch of chilli and some red food colouring. Decorate with dried rose petals.

WHAT THE TESTERS SAY

HATTIE CUFFLIN – 'I gave these to my housemates but added a slug of vodka to my cake mix and the buttercream – they were really colourful and whacky.'

BEN COLEBY – 'I made a batch with fennel and Pernod – I love the mix of sweet and spice.'

TIP

THIS CAKE TASTES BETTER A COUPLE OF DAYS LATER, SO MAKE AHEAD AND STORE IN AN AIRTIGHT CONTAINER.

LEMON OR ORANGE MARZIPAN CAKE

PREPARATION 15 mins | **COOKING** 55 mins–1 hour | **MAKES** 20 cm (8 in) round cake or 20 x 30 cm (8 x 12 in) shallower traybake (8–15 pieces) | **VEGETARIAN**

I have cooked with marzipan (almond paste) for years – filled puff pastry with it to make instant Danish, put it under apples in an apple pie or tart as an instant frangipane and it works brilliantly. Recently, though, I have been a bit more adventurous and have started adding it to recipes for cakes and biscuits – the easiest way to get it into the mix like in this recipe is to grate it. So here is a delectable, sumptuous, very citrussy and very almondy afternoon tea cake – perfect with a cuppa or a very good coffee. I like my lemon/orange zest grated coarsely but you can decide if you prefer it grated finely.

3 lemons or 2 large oranges

175 g (6 oz) butter, at room temperature

100 g (3½ oz/scant ½ cup) caster (superfine) sugar

3 eggs

250 g (9 oz/2 cups) self-raising flour, sifted

250 g (9 oz) ready-made yellow or white marzipan (almond paste), grated

FOR THE ICING

250 g (9 oz/generous 1 cup) icing (confectioners') sugar, sifted

a few drops of lemon juice, fresh or bottled

1. Preheat the oven to 160°C (320°F/Gas 3). Line a cake tin with baking paper.
2. Coarsely grate the lemon or orange zest then, using a serrated knife, remove the pith but not the membrane and chop the flesh finely, discarding any pips. Keep the juice/flesh and zest separately.
3. Put the zest, butter and sugar into a mixing bowl and beat together until pale, smooth and fluffy.
4. Add the eggs and 25 g (1 oz/¼ cup) of the flour and beat again.
5. Add the remaining flour, half the grated marzipan and fruit flesh and juice and mix in with a metal spoon.
6. Turn into the prepared cake tin and sprinkle the rest of the marzipan over. Bake for 55 minutes to 1 hour, or until browned and springy to the touch.
7. This cake is truly moist and can be enjoyed with no topping or you can make a simple icing. Put the icing sugar into a bowl and add a few drops of lemon juice at a time until you get a really thick, spoonable icing. Spoon into the middle of the cake and ease it to the edges using a wet palette knife so that it dribbles over the edges.

WHAT THE TESTERS SAY

JO CURD – 'I don't particularly like marzipan but I loved this really continental-tasting great cake. I used oranges rather than lemons.'

ELLA ARGENTIER – 'I used lemon and orange and doubled the fruit – it was really moist and citrus-tasting.'

BEN COLEBY – 'I have never cooked with marzipan but this worked so well I am inspired to try it in other recipes.'

CHEQUERBOARD CAKE MADE EASY

PREPARATION 30 mins | **COOKING** 20 mins | **MAKES** 1 block cake (8 slices) | **VEGETARIAN** | **NUT-FREE**

Inspired by my nieces, Hattie and Lydia, who made the most beautiful round chequerboard cakes for birthdays last summer, I tried to find a way of getting a similar wow factor but using only one tin. This is perfect for a special tea party. Ideally you need piping bags for this but you can use freezer or greaseproof paper bags and snip the corner off – they need to be quite strong so they don't split. If absolutely necessary, you can just carefully spoon the cake mixture into the tin.

4 eggs
butter, at room temperature
caster (superfine) sugar
self-raising flour
25 g (1 oz/¼ cup) cocoa powder
30 g (1 oz) water
⅓ x 340 g (12 oz) jar apricot jam
Sam's chocolate fudge icing (see page 46) or chocolate ganache (see page 196), to decorate

1. Preheat the oven to 180°C (350°F/Gas 4). Line a roasting or traybake tin with baking paper.
2. Weigh the eggs and in their shells weigh the same amount of butter, sugar and self-raising flour. Beat the butter and sugar together until pale, smooth and fluffy. Add the eggs one at a time, beating well after each addition. (If this curdles then add a spoon of your flour to help it come back together).
3. Sift the flour over the surface and gently fold in using a metal spoon. Now divide the mix equally into 2 bowls. Then spoon 2 tablespoons of mixture from one bowl into the other – this will equal the amounts out when you add the cocoa to the first bowl.
4. Add the cocoa and water to the bowl with less mixture in it and gently fold it in so you now have 2 sponge mixes – one plain and one chocolate. Put the mixture into 2 piping bags (no need for nozzles).
5. Pipe 12 x 20 cm (8 in) long rows alternately one chocolate, one plain, about 2 cm (¾ in) wide and a little apart widthways down the tin so you end up with 12 short rows of mixture. Bake for 15–20 minutes, until the centre springs back when gently pressed or until a cocktail stick inserted in the centre comes out clean. Turn out onto a wire rack and leave to cool.
6. Cut into 3 equal pieces, each of which will have 2 plain and 2 chocolate rows in it. Trim the edges so you have lost the 'thinner' edge bits. Use these for the Leftover Cake Truffles (see page 94).
7. Melt the jam (blend or sieve it if it has lots of fruit bits) and use to sandwich the 3 cakes together. You'll need to turn the middle cake over before sandwiching to make sure the chocolate strips are above the white ones to give the final chequerboard effect.
8. Make either Sam's chocolate fudge icing or chocolate ganache (see pages 46 and 196), spread all over the cake and leave to set. Serve cut in slices.

WHAT THE TESTERS SAY

NAOMI AND RUTH HULME – 'Normally when I have made a Battenburg-type cake I have baked 2 cakes, cut it up and stuck it together but this recipe is great – you only use one tin!'

LYNSEY JONES – 'Cooked this for chalet guests and they loved it.'

HATTIE CUFFLIN – 'A great and easy version of my chequerboard cake – my housemates were impressed!'

TIP
THE CAKE CAN BE MADE AHEAD AND THEN FROZEN. THAW AND DECORATE THE DAY BEFORE NEEDED.

BLACK FOREST GÂTEAU FOR TODAY

PREPARATION 10 mins | **COOKING** 35–40 mins | **MAKES** 1 x 20 cm (8 in) cake (8–10 slices) | **VEGETARIAN** | **NUT-FREE**

When the other Lucy offered me her Lemon Curd Cake recipe for the book (opposite), I immediately loved the idea but sadly had no lemon curd in my cupboard. Instead I made it as a chocolate cake and used blackcurrant jam in place of the curd. The result was a modern version with all the flavours of that 70s classic – Black Forest gâteaux.

175 g (6 oz/¾ cup) caster (superfine) sugar
175 g (6 oz) butter, at room temperature
340 g (12 oz) jar of blackcurrant jam
3 eggs
175 g (6 oz/1½ cups) self-raising flour
50 g (2 oz/scant ½ cup) cocoa powder
icing (confectioners') sugar, for dusting

1. Preheat the oven to 180°C (350°F/Gas 4). Line a 20 cm (8 in) round, deep cake tin with baking paper.
2. Beat the sugar and butter until pale and fluffy then add half the jam. Mix well.
3. Beat in the eggs one at a time, mixing well after each addition.
4. Sift in the flour and cocoa and gently fold in using a metal spoon.
5. Turn the mixture into the prepared tin then drop teaspoons of the remaining jam randomly over the top of the cake.
6. Bake for 35–40 minutes. Allow to cool in the tin, lift out and remove the baking paper. Dust with sifted icing sugar before serving.

WHAT THE TESTERS SAY

BEN COLEBY – 'I added some marinated cherries to the mix and served it with thick Norwegian yoghurt.'

JACK MEEKCOMS – 'I made this with my Dad. We had some really good blackcurrant jam and it was magic the way the jam cooked into the cake.'

LEMON CURD CAKE

PREPARATION	COOKING	MAKES	VEGETARIAN	NUT-FREE
10 mins	35–40 mins	1 x 20 cm (8 in) cake (8–10 slices)		

Here's a lemon cake from Lucy LT that's quick to rustle up, so make sure you always keep a jar of lemon curd in the larder. However, you could lift this cake to something really special by using your own homemade version (see page 192). Try it warm with crème fraîche as a lovely pudding, too.

175 g (6 oz/¾ cup) caster (superfine) sugar
175 g (6 oz) butter, at room temperature
340 g (12 oz) jar of lemon curd (or freshly made, see page 192)
3 eggs
225 g (8 oz/scant 2 cups) self-raising flour
icing (confectioners') sugar, for dusting

1. Preheat the oven to 190°C (375°F/Gas 5). Line a 20 cm (8 in) round, deep cake tin with baking paper.
2. Beat the sugar and butter until well mixed then add half of the jar of lemon curd. Mix well.
3. Beat in the eggs one at a time.
4. Sift over the flour and fold in using a metal spoon.
5. Turn the mixture into the prepared tin then drop teaspoons of the remaining lemon curd randomly over the top of the cake.
6. Bake for 35–40 minutes. Leave the cake to cool in the tin. Turn out, remove the baking paper and dust with sifted icing sugar.

WHAT THE TESTERS SAY

LIZ EVERSON – 'I thought the mixture was too dry before I baked it but resisted adding anything and when it came out is was soft and sweet and succulent. My husband Noel enjoyed his slice warm with ice cream.'

STELLA CAUDWELL – 'A really easy, lovely continental sort of cake, which we had for pudding as well as with a cup of coffee.'

CLAIRE VAN DIJK – 'This cake is great – can't say any more than that – worth buying good lemon curd though and make sure your oven is up to temperature before baking.'

TIP
THE MIXTURE ALSO MAKES GREAT LITTLE CUPCAKES.

15-MINUTE MUFFINS

PREPARATION	COOKING	MAKES	VEGETARIAN	NUT-FREE
2 mins	15 mins	8–10 large muffins		(basic recipe only)

If you are a morning muffin fan and have never made them then get baking. You do not even need scales for this one – simply use the yoghurt pot to measure the rest of the ingredients. You can have them in the oven in a couple of minutes and they take 15 minutes to bake – on a weekend what could be more enticing than the smell of homemade muffins coming out of the oven? If you only have a large pot of yoghurt, then weigh 125 g (4 oz/½ cup) into a ramekin and then measure the rest at the same level in that – this is about volume not weight.

FOR BASIC MUFFINS
125 g (4 oz) individual pot of plain yoghurt
  (keep the pot to measure the remaining ingredients)
2 yoghurt pots of sunflower or vegetable oil
2 yoghurt pots of caster (superfine) sugar
3 yoghurt pots of self-raising flour
4 eggs

1 Preheat the oven to 180°C (350°F/Gas 4). Line a large muffin tin with 8 muffin papers (if you add other flavours, see opposite variations, it will make up to 10 muffins).
2 Scoop the yoghurt into a mixing bowl then measure in the oil, sugar and flour.
3 Add the eggs and mix to a smooth batter.
4 Spoon the mixture in the muffin cases, three-quarters full, and bake for 15 minutes or until cracked and browned on the top. Serve warm or cool on a wire rack.

VARIATIONS

APPLE AND CINNAMON – Grate 1 apple into the basic mixture and add 3 g (⅛ oz) cinnamon to the mix. Slice a second apple, laying the slices on the top of the muffin mixture in the cases before baking.

SOUR CHERRY AND WHITE CHOCOLATE – Add 100 g (3½ oz) chopped white chocolate and 50 g (2 oz) dried sour cherries to the basic mixture.

DOUBLE CHOCOLATE CHIP – Substitute 20 g (¾ oz/ scant ¼ cup) flour with the same amount of cocoa powder in the basic mixture and throw in 50 g (2 oz) each of chopped white and milk chocolate.

LEMON DRIZZLE – Add the grated zest of 1 lemon to the mixture, bake as before and, while hot, spoon over 200 g (7 oz/1⅔ cups) icing (confectioners') sugar mixed with the juice of the lemon.

CARROT AND WALNUT – Finely grate 1 carrot and add to the basic mixture with a pinch of ground cinnamon, a pinch of ground ginger and 50 g (2 oz) chopped walnuts. When cool, top with the cream cheese frosting on page 197.

WHAT THE TESTERS SAY

HARRY AND MIA ROGERS – 'We made apple and cinnamon muffins with a slice of apple on the top of each, which looked great.'

SARA MCDONALD – 'I love this recipe – no weighing required! I split my batch and did 2 flavours of muffins for my friends in one bake!'

BANANA AND PASSION FRUIT CAKE

PREPARATION	COOKING	MAKES	VEGETARIAN	NUT-FREE
15 mins	35 mins	1 x 20 cm (8 in) cake (8 slices)		

This gorgeous cake is absolutely perfect for any grown-up special occasion. The passion fruit adds a zing and a crunch to the sweet banana cake and the buttercream is to die for. It's worth investing in piping bags and a fluted nozzle for this one, for an extra special look, but you can, of course, simply pile the buttercream on if you prefer and swirl it around with a palette knife. Dribble extra passion fruit pulp over for a real shot of colour. The mixture can be made into cupcakes too.

4 ripe bananas
125 g (4 oz) butter, at room temperature
225 g (8 oz/1 cup) caster (superfine) sugar
2 large eggs
2 passion fruit
225 g (8 oz/1¾ cups) self-raising flour
icing (confectioners') sugar, for dusting

FOR THE BUTTERCREAM

125 g (4 oz) butter, at room temperature
5 g (¼ oz) orange extract
250 g (9 oz/2 cups) icing (confectioners') sugar, sifted
2 passion fruit
5 g (¼ oz) lemon juice

1. Preheat the oven to 180°C (350°F/Gas 4). Line a 20 cm (8 in) round, deep cake tin with baking paper.
2. Put the ripe bananas into the bowl and mix with a fork or electric mixer until a rough paste. Throw in the butter and sugar and mix again until smoothish.
3. Add the eggs and mix again.
4. Scoop the flesh and pips out of the 2 passion fruit and add both to the bowl. Using a metal spoon, fold these into the mixture with the flour.
5. Spoon the mixture into the cake tin, level the surface and bake for 35 minutes or until springy when lightly pressed. The cooked cake can be cooled then frozen at this stage or stored in an airtight container for up to a week before decorating.
6. Make the buttercream by beating the butter, orange extract and icing sugar together. Spoon a third of the plain buttercream into a piping bag or set aside in a bowl for spreading later. Stir the flesh and pips of the 2 passion fruit into the rest of the buttercream. Add the lemon juice to taste.
7. Cut the cold cake in half horizontally and lift the top half off by sliding a flat baking sheet between the 2 halves. While the top half of the cake is off, dust with icing sugar and pipe 12 rosettes with the plain buttercream or simply spread the top with buttercream if you have no piping bag.
8. Mix any leftover plain buttercream into the passion fruit icing. Spread liberally over the cut surface of the bottom half of the cake and then carefully slide the top cake back in position.

WHAT THE TESTERS SAY

IRENE O'SULLIVAN – 'This is really delicious and guaranteed to disappear fast.'

TOM ROBERTS – 'Excellent – I made it with non-dairy ingredients for my daughter with a dairy intolerance.'

CLAIRE VAN DIJK – 'I made this for Mother's Day – it is a perfect cake for special occasions and I loved the tangy passion fruit with the rich banana.'

TIP
THE BANANAS MUST BE REALLY RIPE OR THE TEXTURE OF THE CAKE WILL BE A BIT CHEWY AND LACK TRUE BANANA FLAVOUR AND SWEETNESS.

What's the difference between a cookie and a biscuit? Sounds like the beginning of a joke, but seriously the only difference I can find is that most cookie recipes contain an egg and most biscuit recipes do not. In my head, cookies are larger and chewy and biscuits are crunchier. Whether there are technical differences or not, we all know what we are talking about and in this chapter I know you will find biscuits and cookies you will make over and over again – yum! For extra tips and ideas before you start see page 8.

COOKIES AND BISCUITS

ALMOND THINS

PREPARATION	COOKING	MAKES	VEGETARIAN
10 mins + chilling	10 mins	about 30 little thins	

From an old French/Belgian recipe, these utterly nutty little thin biscuits are perfect to serve with after-dinner coffee or to accompany any fruit dessert, ice cream or mousse. Although they are simple to make, you need to allow time to chill the mixture in the freezer; it needs to be hard so it can be sliced thinly and these biscuits are meant to be really thin!

60 g (2 oz) butter
25 g (1 oz) water
180 g (6 oz/generous ¾ cup) demerara (raw) sugar
80 g (3 oz/scant 1 cup) flaked almonds
3 g (⅛ oz) ground cinnamon
5 g (¼ oz) vanilla extract
150 g (5 oz/1¼ cups) plain (all-purpose) flour

1. Line a loaf tin with a double thickness of cling film (plastic wrap).
2. Simply melt the butter, water and sugar together in a saucepan – do not boil.
3. Add the almonds, cinnamon, vanilla and flour – stir well and mix into a soft dough.
4. Press the dough into the tin, flattening the top and cover with the cling film. Preheat the oven to 180°C (350°F/Gas 4).
5. Pop the tin into the freezer for at least 20 minutes or until firm enough to slice very thinly (use a sharp knife). Slice as thinly and evenly as you can. Cut off as many biscuits as you want to bake and return the rest to the freezer for another day. Place the biscuits on baking sheets lined with baking paper.
6. Bake for 10 minutes, or until golden brown all over – they will crisp up as they cool. Cool on the sheets for a little while, then slide the paper on to wire racks to cool completely. Try not to eat them all before it's time to serve them – oh so easy to do! They are perfect with ice cream. Store any leftover ones in an airtight container.

WHAT THE TESTERS SAY

IAN MEEKCOMS – 'Really moreish and easy to make. We ate them with strong black coffee – excellent!'

RON SAWERS – 'Easy to make with a really professional-looking biscuit when baked.'

NAOMI HULME – 'A lovely, fine after-dinner biscuit. I have the frozen dough in my freezer so I can simply bake a few when friends come round – a great thing.'

TIP

YOU CAN SIMPLY MAKE THE DOUGH, CHILL IT AS PER THE METHOD ABOVE, SLICE OFF AND BAKE WHAT YOU NEED. WRAP THE REMAINING MIX AND STORE IN THE FREEZER.

TORTAS DE ACEITE

PREPARATION 40 mins (includes proving) | **COOKING** 5 mins | **MAKES** about 12 tortas | **VEGAN & VEGETARIAN** | **NUT-FREE** | **DAIRY-FREE**

The other Lucy has visited the island of Majorca many times and she always returns with one very special thing – a packet of Tortas de Aceite. *She brings them round and we devour them while swapping cooking tales and holiday stories over coffee. She has spent a long time perfecting them at home. These 'biscuits' are actually thin, crisp pastries that originated in Andalucia. They are an interesting alternative to serve with creamy possets or tangy fresh fruit salad.*

90 g (3 oz) warm water
10 g (½ oz) fast-action (instant) dried yeast
5 g (¼ oz) salt
25 g (1 oz/⅛ cup) caster (superfine) sugar
75 g (2½ oz) Spanish olive oil
300 g (10½ oz/2½ cups) plain (all-purpose) flour
granulated sugar, for topping
anise or caraway seeds, for topping

1. In a large mixing bowl, mix the warm water with the yeast, salt, caster sugar and olive oil.
2. Gradually add the flour, mixing thoroughly. If the dough mixture becomes too dry to work, sprinkle in a bit more water and mix until the dough has a smooth consistency.
3. Cover the bowl with a tea towel and leave in a warm place for 30 minutes or until doubled in bulk.
4. Preheat the oven to 230°C (450°F/Gas 8). Cover 2 baking sheets with baking paper.
5. Turn the proved dough out onto a floured board. Pinch off 40 g (1½ oz) of dough and roll into a ball. Place on the prepared baking sheet and flatten the dough slightly then, using a rolling pin, roll the dough out until very thin, to about 15 cm (6 in) in diameter.
6. Sprinkle generously with granulated sugar and a scattering of the seeds. Repeat with a second piece of the dough.
7. Bake one above the other for 5 minutes and then take a look at the tortas. They should be bubbled, crisp and dry with the majority of the sugar melted with some really toasty, burnt bits of caramel. If necessary, swap the sheets over and return to the oven, checking every couple of minutes.
8. Cool on a wire rack as you roll more *tortas*. As soon as they are cool, put into an airtight container layered with the baking paper they were cooked on. The tortas will only keep for a day or so in their airtight container but are very moreish, so storage is not really a problem!

WHAT THE TESTERS SAY

CATHERINE DOEL – 'I love these tortas and they were easy enough to do once I got the baking timings right. Don't know why they're so expensive in the shops as the ingredients were very cheap!'

IAN MEEKCOMS – 'Definitely one of my favourites – I really love the dark caramel flavours.'

BEN COLEBY – 'I love fennel and was intrigued by this recipe as I did not know what they were at all. I found it a bit hard to get the temperature right for baking but now I can churn them out, so I am going to try flavouring them with cardamom next.'

TIP

DEEP-FLAVOURED SPANISH OLIVE OIL IS TRADITIONALLY USED BUT YOU CAN USE WHICHEVER OLIVE OIL YOU PREFER (OR HAVE IN YOUR CUPBOARD).

CLASSIC CRUNCHY BISCUITS

PREPARATION 5 mins | **COOKING** 10 mins | **MAKES** 10 biscuits | **VEGETARIAN** | **NUT-FREE**

Crispy, crunchy and very moreish – these will become a biscuit that you make over and over. I took batches of the raw cookie dough into the Skiworld London with a large box of extra ingredients. Everyone set about creating their 'signature' cookie. We had a huge bake off and an even more enormous 'tasting' session (there are 40 staff!). Ollie de le Vingne, operations manager, won with his inspired fresh lime, chilli and ginger. Try the top combinations opposite, (or use the soft cookie ones on page 78). I use Lyle's golden syrup as it is made from sugar cane and has a better flavour.

75 g (2½ oz) butter, at room temperature
few drops of vanilla extract
75 g (2½ oz/⅓ cup) caster (superfine) sugar
75 g (2½ oz) golden (corn) syrup
125 g (4 oz/1 cup) self-raising flour
5 g (¼ oz) bicarbonate of soda (baking soda)

1. Preheat the oven to 190°C (375°F/Gas 5). Line 2 baking sheets with baking paper.
2. Beat the butter, vanilla, sugar and syrup together until creamy.
3. Sift over the flour and bicarbonate of soda and mix well to a stiff dough. Add any 'extras' (see alternatives opposite, or ones of your own) and work in by hand.
4. With wet hands, roll the dough into 30 g (1 oz) balls. Flatten slightly, then place onto the prepared baking sheets. Leave room for the cookies to spread. (I bake 5 per sheet.)
5. Bake for 10 minutes for a crunchy biscuit. Transfer to a wire rack to cool.
6. Store in an airtight container for up to 1 week.

TIP

TRY USING DARK BROWN SUGAR IN PLACE OF CASTER (SUPERFINE) SUGAR TO GET THE FLAVOUR OF MOLASSES — IT'S GREAT WITH FLAVOURINGS SUCH AS GINGER.

LUCY'S BAKES

ALTERNATIVES

OLLIE'S PRIZE-WINNING LIME, CHILLI AND GINGER – add 20 g (¾ oz) ground ginger, 150 g (5 oz) chopped, crystallised ginger, finely grated zest of 1 lime and 4 g (¼ oz) dried chilli flakes.

WHITE CHOCOLATE AND CRANBERRY – add 100 g (3½ oz) chopped white chocolate and 50 g (2 oz) chopped dried cranberries.

CAPPUCCINO – add 4 whole coffee beans, toasted and chopped or crushed and 50 g (2 oz) white chocolate, chopped.

DARK CHOCOLATE AND HAZELNUT – add 50 g (2 oz) dark chocolate, chopped and 50 g (2 oz) hazelnuts, chopped.

ORANGE ZEST AND CINNAMON – add the grated zest of 1 orange and 3 g (⅛ oz) ground cinnamon.

TURKISH DELIGHT – add 50 g (2 oz) of Turkish delight, chopped and 5 g (¼ oz) rose water.

BOUNTY – add 2 small Bounty bars (a 57 g/ 2½ oz pack), chopped.

WHAT THE THE TESTERS SAY

KERRY GREGORY – 'I made them with white and milk chocolate buttons and shared with family and friends – they didn't last long. They are really adaptable and you could add any of your favourite bits, so they should be re-named The World's Best Biscuits!'

IAN MEEKCOMS – 'A great one to make with the kids.'

JO CURD – 'I used half the syrup and preferred them – my son's friends were at our house and they demolished the lot!'

MY BEST GINGER SNAPS

PREPARATION 15 mins | **COOKING** 10 mins | **MAKES** about 15 snaps | **VEGETARIAN** | **NUT-FREE**

My mother was a cake and biscuit maker, so there was usually something homemade about when I was growing up, but we also had a biscuit tin full of shop-bought favourites – HobNobs, chocolate digestives and ginger nuts. I was the ginger nut fan. In my mind ginger nuts are made for dunking. This is a crispy, hard biscuit with a real ginger punch. Using bicarbonate of soda (baking soda) as well as the self-raising flour gives them the crinkly top as they rise and then fall.

50 g (2 oz) butter
50 g (2 oz/¼ cup) soft light brown or caster (superfine) sugar
100 g (3½ oz) golden (corn) syrup
125 g (4 oz/1 cup) self-raising flour
8 g (⅓ oz) bicarbonate of soda (baking soda)
15 g (½ oz) ground ginger

1. Preheat the oven to 190°C (375°F/Gas 5). Line 2 baking sheets with baking paper.
2. In a mixing bowl, beat the butter, sugar and syrup together until well mixed using a wooden spoon or electric whisk.
3. Add the rest of the ingredients and keep mixing until you have a stiff dough – it will go crumbly at first then gradually come together.
4. Wet your hands and roll into about 15 x 30 g (1 oz) balls, flattening each between your palms before placing them on the baking sheets. Leave enough room for the biscuits to spread. Wet your hands again between each biscuit to stop them sticking to you.
5. Bake for 10 minutes or until browned, swapping the sheets over half way through cooking.
6. Allow to cool on the baking sheets or on a wire rack. These will crisp up as they cool. Store in an airtight container.

WHAT THE TESTERS SAY

STELLA CAUDWELL – 'My husband enjoyed them with coffee and my playing partners enjoyed them during a round of golf! I tried different sizes and think a 15–20 g (½–¾ oz) ball is ideal.'

RON SAWERS – 'These baked beautifully in the Aga and I was really impressed with how similar they were to shop-bought ones! I shared them with neighbours who did not believe I had made them.'

ANTONIA ARGENTIER – 'We cannot buy ginger nuts in France so I was very keen to make these and they did not disappoint. I dunk mine!'

TIP
I BUY MY GROUND GINGER FROM A LOCAL ASIAN GROCER SHOP BECAUSE IT IS MUCH BETTER VALUE, BUT I ALSO THINK IT IS HOTTER AND SPICIER.

HOMEMADE HOBNOBS

PREPARATION	COOKING	MAKES	VEGETARIAN	NUT-FREE
15 mins	12–15 mins	15 biscuits		

These crunchy biscuits are based on my beloved HobNobs. They're buttery, sweet and crunchy with a tiny nod to health by adding a few jumbo oats. Lyle's golden syrup is made with sugar cane and I think this is a better flavour than sugar beet syrups. Check the label of the brand you choose to see which type of sugar it is made from.

170 g (6 oz) butter, at room temperature
60 g (2 oz) golden (corn) syrup
120 g (4 oz/gernerous ½ cup) demerara (raw) sugar, plus extra for coating
5 g (¼ oz) vanilla extract
200 g (7 oz) self-raising flour
60 g (2 oz/⅔ cup) jumbo (large) rolled oats

1. Preheat the oven to 190°C (375°F/Gas 5). Line 2 baking sheets with baking paper.
2. Beat the butter, syrup, sugar and vanilla together in a mixing bowl until creamy, using a wooden spoon or an electric hand whisk.
3. Add the dry ingredients and mix to a firm dough. Roll into a sausage approximately 6 cm (2½ in) diameter. Roll the log in a little extra demerara so it is coated all the way round. Wrap in cling film (plastic wrap) and chill for 30 minutes. Slice into ½–1 cm (¼–½ in) thick rounds.
4. Lay the biscuits on the prepared baking sheets and bake for 12–15 minutes, until golden, swapping the sheets over half way through cooking.
5. Cool on a wire rack (they will crisp as they cool) and store in an airtight container.

WHAT THE TESTERS SAY

THE ROBINSON FAMILY – 'My children prefer softer cookies and these are a crunchy biscuit, but I shared them with friends and we loved them.'

MAURICE FLYNN – 'I had everything I needed in the cupboard just waiting for this recipe! I added cinnamon as I love the smell of it baking but could have added mixed peel, dried fruit or candied peel.'

HATTIE CUFFLIN – 'I made them and ate them warm – just great!'

TIP

IF YOU WANT A REAL COFFEE HIT THEN ADD MORE COFFEE GRANULES BUT KEEP THE WATER THE SAME.

COFFEE AND CARDAMOM BISCUITS

PREPARATION 10 mins | **COOKING** 8–9 mins | **MAKES** about 12 biscuits | **VEGETARIAN** | **NUT-FREE**

At a grand cookie and biscuit bake off at the Skiworld London office, Emily Chew created a coffee and cardamom flavoured crunchy biscuit using the batches of basic dough I took in (see page 72). The taste was divine but because we needed to tweak all the ingredients to add the liquid coffee and still get the right texture, we decided it deserved a recipe of its own. It's a really grown-up biscuit for coffee lovers with a hint of foreign flavours that is quite magical.

6–8 cardamom pods
10–15 g (½ oz) instant coffee granules
30 g (1 oz) boiling water
50 g (2 oz) butter, at room temperature
75 g (2½ oz/⅓ cup) caster (superfine) sugar
50 g (2 oz) golden (corn) syrup
175 g (6 oz/scant 1½ cups) self-raising flour
9 g (½ oz) bicarbonate of soda (baking soda)

1. Preheat the oven to 190°C (375°F/Gas 5). Line a baking sheet with baking paper.
2. Split the cardamom pods, remove the seeds and make sure they are all separated by rubbing them in between your fingers.
3. Dissolve the coffee in the water.
4. Add the butter, sugar, syrup and cardamom seeds and beat together with a wooden spoon or electric mixer until smooth.
5. Sift over the flour and bicarbonate of soda and mix well until combined. This may be crumbly at first but then work with your hands to form a firm dough.
6. Roll the dough into 20 g (¾ oz) balls and put them onto the lined baking sheet with space in between.
7. Wet your hands and flatten the cookies to about 5 mm (¼ in) thick. Bake for 8–9 minutes depending how crunchy you like them.
8. Transfer to a wire rack to cool and get the crispiest biscuit you can.
9. Store in an airtight container for up to 2 weeks.

WHAT THE TESTERS SAY

SAM RAFTER – 'I'm a real coffee freak and a big fan of spiced biscuits, and these were great with a coffee.'

CATHERINE DOEL – 'These easy-to-make biscuits have a great flavour combination and keep well when stored in an airtight tin (but you need to hide the tin!).'

BRENDAN CROFT – 'I made these with a gluten-free flour blend and they worked well, but then I made them with wheat flour and added even more coffee for a big coffee hit – I love them dunked.'

| VEGETARIAN | NUT-FREE |

SOFT COOKIES

PREPARATION 5 mins | **COOKING** 8–10 mins | **MAKES** 12 large cookies

The American-style of soft cookie has become really popular over the last 15 years in the UK and here is the recipe I use as a base for all my soft cookies. As I mentioned before, I took a massive batch of dough into the Skiworld office and bags of 'extras' and everyone had a go at creating their signature cookie. Ryan Chitty in marketing won the soft cookie tasting with his coconut and Daim – his and a few of the other winning combinations are here for you to try (you can also use the Classic Crunchy Biscuits flavour combinations on page 72). Don't hold back on the salt in this recipe!

125 g (4 oz) butter, at room temperature
5 g (¼ oz) vanilla extract
pinch of salt
225 g (8 oz/1 cup) caster (superfine) sugar
1 egg
225 g (8 oz/1¾ cups) self-raising flour
5 g (¼ oz) bicarbonate of soda (baking soda)

1. Preheat the oven to 190°C (375°F/Gas 5). Line 2 or 3 baking sheets with baking paper.
2. Beat the butter, vanilla, salt, sugar and egg together until well-mixed.
3. Add the flour and bicarbonate of soda and mix well to a stiff dough. Add any extras flavours (see opposite), or ones of your own, and work in by hand.
4. With wet hands, roll the dough into 12 x 50 g (2 oz) balls. Flatten between your palms to about 5 mm (¼ in) thick then place well apart, to allow for spreading, on the prepared baking sheets. Bake for 8 minutes for very soft cookies and up to 9–10 minutes for slightly crisper ones. Cool on a wire rack then store in an airtight container for up to 1 week.

ALTERNATIVES ←

RYAN CHITTY'S WINNING DAIM AND COCONUT COMBO – replace 50 g (2 oz) flour with 50 g (2 oz) desiccated coconut, and add 3 Daim bars, chopped.

JENNY GREENWOOD'S WERTHER – add 50 g (2 oz) Werther's Original sweets, crushed.

CHOCOLATE CHIP – add 100 g (3½ oz) chocolate chips or chopped chocolate of your choice.

DOUBLE CHOCOLATE CHIP – Replace 25 g (1 oz) flour with 25 g (1 oz) cocoa in the mix and add 100 g (3½ oz) chocolate chips.

CHOCOLATE/ORANGE – omit the vanilla extract and add 100 g (3½ oz) chocolate chips and the finely grated zest of 1 orange.

RAISIN AND ORANGE – omit the vanilla and add the finely grated zest of 1 orange and 100 g (3½ oz) raisins.

WHAT THE TESTERS SAY ←

HANNAH, AJ AND MADDY CUFFLIN – 'We are American so this is what we call a cookie. We weighed them in at 65 g (2¼ oz) and they were BIG. We added a ton of M&M's to ours – yum!'

JOSH AND BEN CURD – 'We made lots of these and they lasted no time in our tin – we have friends round often so they are a great thing to have to hand.'

COLIN MEEKCOMS – 'I am a novice baker – I followed the recipe and I thought they could not make a cookie when I put them in the oven, but they set as they cooled and transformed into real American-style soft cookies – I am so proud!'

TIP
IF YOU LOAD THE OVEN WITH MORE THAN A COUPLE OF TRAYS OF COOKIES YOU MAY NEED TO EXTEND THE COOKING TIME SLIGHTLY.

MY MUM'S VIENNESE BISCUITS

PREPARATION 15 mins | **COOKING** 10–15 mins | **MAKES** 15 large-size biscuits | **VEGETARIAN** | **NUT-FREE**

When we were small, one of my strongest memories of home is rows and rows of fruits loaves and these Viennese biscuits lined up on the kitchen table ready for packing up for bazaars, fêtes and charity functions – mum was always baking for something. We were always allowed to help dip the ends in the chocolate or even pipe the mixture, which was great because we got to eat the breakages, and of course, lick the bowl. A baking book in my mind would be missing something if these classic little biscuits were not among its pages. You will make them again and again!

200 g (7 oz) salted butter, at room temperature
80 g (3 oz) icing (confectioners') sugar
200 g (7 oz) plain (all-purpose) flour
25 g (1 oz) cornflour
200 g (7 oz) plain or milk chocolate

1. Line a baking tray with baking paper and heat the oven to 190°C (375°F/Gas 5).
2. Using an electric whisk, beat the butter and icing sugar together until really soft and creamy.
3. Add the flour and cornflour and mix by hand at first so the flour does not fly everywhere, then using the electric whisk, beat to a soft dough (the dough should be soft enough to pipe).
4. Carefully spoon the mixture into the piping bag and pipe sausages of mixture onto the tray, leaving about 3 cm (1¼ in) between the biscuits.
5. Bake for 10–15 minutes, or until golden brown. Leave to cool for a few minutes on the tray then transfer to a wire rack.
6. When they are completely cold melt the chocolate in a bowl over a pan of boiling water. Dip each end of the biscuits into the melted chocolate. Leave the biscuits to set on a sheet of baking paper so they do not stick.
7. Store in an airtight tin for up to 2 weeks.

WHAT THE TESTERS SAY

MANDY FISHER – 'I am not accomplished with a piping bag but I used some sturdy disposable ones and bought myself a metal nozzle. They were better at the end of the batch than at the beginning. Next time I think they will look quite professional!'

MICHAEL CUFFLIN (AGED 13) – 'I love having my own piping stuff in the kitchen drawer. It was hard to start with but after a few tries, my biscuits were great – I put lots of chocolate on them.'

LIZ EVERSON – 'I actually managed to dig out a piping bag from the 80s and I did not find the piping very hard. I coated the ends with dark chocolate.'

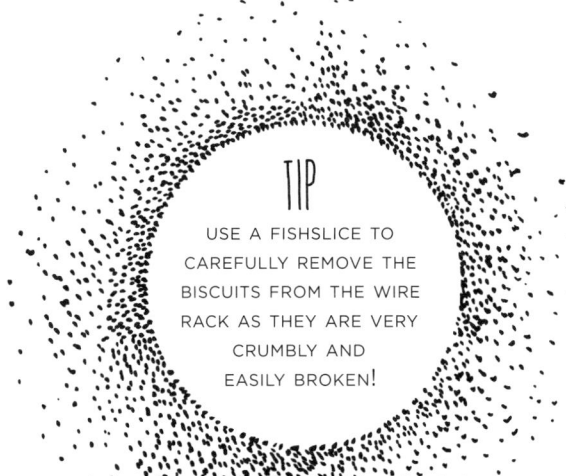

TIP: USE A FISHSLICE TO CAREFULLY REMOVE THE BISCUITS FROM THE WIRE RACK AS THEY ARE VERY CRUMBLY AND EASILY BROKEN!

There is not much that says you love someone or care about them more than a homemade, edible gift. Here is a selection of ideas for delicious, frivolous sweet treats that you can wrap up as presents, share with friends or simply save as a secret little luxury for yourself on a rainy day...because you're worth it. Before you pop on your chef's hat see page 8 for extra tips, tricks, advice and kitchen secrets.

SWEET TREATS

TIP
FOR A SHORTCUT, USE SALTED ROASTED NUTS — NO NEED TO TOAST THESE — THEY ADD A SALTINESS TO THE BRITTLE WHICH I REALLY LIKE.

NUT BRITTLE

| PREPARATION | COOKING | MAKES | VEGETARIAN | DAIRY- |
| 15 mins | 5 mins | 1 x 20 cm tin (8 in) | | FREE |

I stayed some years ago on the Greek island of Symi; we walked all over the island taking our lunch to enjoy in quiet bays. It is really hard to find something sweet to take as it is so hot and food melts, but they sell wonderful pistachio brittle, which is perfect in hot weather! When we returned to the UK, I set about making some brittle and soon decided that many recipes had too much caramel for me – what I like is lots of nuts with just enough dark caramel to hold them together. You can use any nuts – toast them first for the best flavour and texture.

300 g (10½ oz) mixed nuts of your choice
80 g (3 oz) water
250 g (9 oz) granulated sugar
good pinch of salt

1. Preheat the oven to 190°C (375°F/Gas 5). Line a 20 cm (8 in) shallow baking tin with baking paper.
2. Bake the nuts on a baking sheet for 7 minutes, or until browned but not too dark. Remove from the oven and set aside to cool.
3. While these are cooking, put the water and sugar into a saucepan and heat very gently until the sugar has completely dissolved, stirring from time to time. Do not allow to boil at this stage.
4. When the sugar is dissolved, turn up the heat and bring to the boil. It will bubble a lot – this is the water evaporating and this must happen for the sugar to get to a high enough temperature to caramelise. Stir from time to time.
5. It will start to change colour, stir gently and watch it change from pale gold to a medium brown – you can smell the caramel as it turns. You need it a nutty brown colour so it has a hint of bitterness, but do not allow to burn. As soon as it is ready, throw in the nuts and salt, stir quickly and turn the mixture into the prepared tin. Leave to go completely cold and hard.
6. Using a small hammer or a rolling pin, break the brittle into bite-sized pieces for eating, or crush in a thick plastic bag to make praline to sprinkle on cakes or desserts.

WHAT THE TESTERS SAY

BEN COLEBY – 'I used pistachio nuts to make my brittle – I know nothing about caramel but I managed the recipe without a disaster, but you definitely need to wait until it smells a bit burnt before you put the nuts in or it is a sweet, sticky mess.'

HATTIE CUFFLIN – 'I love this – I made my caramel quite dark and I think that is what gives it flavour, so don't take it off the heat too soon.'

SIMON EBBS – 'I love anything nutty but had never made nut brittle before – it turns out it is nothing to be scared of!'

HATTIE'S CHOCOLATE FUDGE

PREPARATION	COOKING	MAKES	VEGETARIAN	GLUTEN-FREE
10 mins + chilling	about 5 mins	64–100 squares (depending on size)		

My lovely niece, Hattie, has adored baking and cooking since she was a tiny dot. One Christmas, when she cannot have been more than about 6 years old, she produced a plate piled high with her homemade chocolate fudge. I am not sure where she came across the recipe but she made it on her own, and made it again and again to the delight of us all! It has become a family tradition at gatherings – thanks Hats!

25 g (1 oz) butter
250 g (9 oz) dark chocolate
50 g (2 oz) milk
50 g (2 oz) full-fat cream cheese
5 g (¼ oz) vanilla extract
450 g (1 lb) icing (confectioner's) sugar, sifted
125 g (4 oz) chopped toasted nuts (optional)

1. Line a 20 cm (8 in) square tin with baking paper.
2. Put the butter, chocolate, milk and cream cheese into a saucepan and melt it together over a low heat. This will be a thick mixture. Stir it all the time.
3. Once melted, boil for 1 minute and keep stirring. Add the vanilla and icing sugar, stir well and boil again for 1 minute – the mixture should be very thick and sticky. Add the nuts, if using.
4. Turn the mixture into the prepared tin, spread it out evenly using a wet palette knife and chill for at least 4 hours, or overnight.
5. Cut into squares. Store in an airtight container.

WHAT THE TESTERS SAY

LYDIA CUFFLIN AND SIMON CHILDS – 'We made some and took it to friends at the weekend – we added 10 g (½ oz) cocoa powder on the second batch to make it even more chocolatey.'

ANTONIA ARGENTIER – 'The mixture was really stiff in the saucepan but I boiled it for the stated time and the result was amazing. I am going to make it for gifts for Christmas as I live in France and fudge is quite unusual here.'

CATHERINE AND MATTHEW SELLS – 'Brilliantly easy and delicious!'

OH-SO-EASY PEANUT BUTTER FUDGE

PREPARATION	COOKING	MAKES	VEGETARIAN	GLUTEN-FREE
2 mins + cooling	10 mins	about 28 squares		

Well, the other Lucy has been making this fudge for many of our catering functions for years and although it tastes nutty you would not necessarily pin the taste down to peanut butter. Salty, sweet and utterly moreish, it's a winner every time. The only thing to watch is not to let the sugar mixture boil before the sugar is dissolved or it will form into hard crystals. The fudge, apart from devouring or giving as gifts, of course, is very good chopped small and used to decorate chocolate cakes and muffins.

50 g (2 oz) butter
200 g (7 oz/generous 1 cup) demerara (raw) or soft brown sugar
50 g (2 oz) milk
100 g (3½ oz) peanut butter
3 g (⅛ oz) vanilla extract
120 g (4oz/1 cup) icing (confectioners') sugar, sifted

1. Line a 1 kg (2 lb) loaf tin with baking paper.
2. Put the butter, sugar and milk in a large saucepan over a gentle heat. Stir very gently until the all the sugar has dissolved.
3. Once the sugar has dissolved, bring to the boil and, without stirring, cook for 3 minutes. Remove from the heat and stir in the peanut butter and vanilla extract.
4. When well mixed, add the sifted icing sugar, stir in and then beat with a wooden spoon until the fudge is nice and smooth.
5. Spoon the fudge into the prepared tin, level the surface and leave to cool, uncovered.
6. Lift out the fudge in its paper and cut into neat, even squares.
7. Store in an airtight container or put into jars if using for gifts.

WHAT THE TESTERS SAY

MARCELLA SCOTT – 'Ace recipe – you need some strong arms towards the end for stirring but it's a joy to make. I like to leave my fudge plain – I put 4 squares in little bags and gave them as presents.'

SAMUEL RAFTER – 'Anything with peanut butter in it or on it is fine by me. I do not eat fudge generally but this is really salty and I loved that. I would definitely make it again.'

STELLA CAUDWELL – 'I first had this when Lucy LT gave me a box of it for my birthday – I loved it and I love the easy recipe.'

TIP
TO MAKE A CHOCOLATE VERSION, ADD 50 G (2 OZ) MELTED CHOCOLATE TO THE ICING (CONFECTIONERS') SUGAR.

TIP

THE FUDGE CAN BE MADE UP TO TWO WEEKS AHEAD, SO PLAN IT INTO YOUR PRE-CHRISTMAS COOKING FOR GIFTS OR IF YOU WANT TO SERVE IT ON A SPECIAL DATE.

Clockwise from the top: Oh-So-Easy Peanut Butter Fudge; Hattie's Chocolate Fudge

SOUR CHERRY MINI FLORENTINES

PREPARATION 10 mins + cooking | **COOKING** 10–12 mins | **MAKES** about 30 | **VEGETARIAN**

I was reacquainted with a childhood friend on a social networking site recently and she said that it was not a surprise to her that I cook for a living. She remembered when we took our Brownie cooking badge she cooked fairy cakes and I turned up and cooked Cornish pasties from scratch and Florentines – we were 10 years old! So here is that same recipe. I am not a huge lover of candied peel (usually found in Florentines) so I simply miss that out. As long as the combination of fruit and nuts in this recipe totals 200 g (7 oz), you can add whichever ones you like best.

25 g (1 oz) salted butter
65 g (2½ oz) double (heavy) cream
75 g (2½ oz/⅓ cup) caster (superfine) sugar
15 g (½ oz/⅛ cup) plain (all-purpose) flour
100 g (3½ oz/generous 1 cup) flaked almonds
50 g (2 oz/generous ⅓ cup) pistachios or hazelnuts, chopped
50 g (2 oz) dried sour cherries, chopped
175 g (6 oz) dark chocolate

1. Preheat the oven to 190°C (375°F/Gas 5). Line a baking sheet with baking paper.
2. Melt the butter, cream and sugar in a saucepan. Stir in the flour and then the rest of the ingredients. Set aside to cool.
3. Place small teaspoons of the mix onto the prepared baking sheet, flatten them as much as you can and leave a 2 cm (¾ in) gap between each as they will spread. As you flatten it does not matter if there are little holes in the mixture as they will fill out.
4. Bake for 10–12 minutes or until an evenly medium golden brown colour, then remove from the oven and leave for a couple of minutes until firm enough to remove. Cool on a wire rack, then transfer to a sheet of baking paper, inverting the Florentines so the smooth underside is uppermost.
5. Melt the chocolate either in the microwave on a medium-low setting or in a bowl over a pan of boiling water and spread the underside of each Florentine with chocolate. Wait until nearly set then, using a fork, mark wave shapes into the chocolate – this is traditional decoration for a Florentine but not compulsory!
6. When completely cold, store in an airtight container. Eat within a week.

WHAT THE TESTERS SAY

DI PALUMBO – 'You never see these in cake shop windows anymore! I used 70 per cent chocolate and a mix of hazelnuts and walnuts for a really bitter after dinner treat.'

BEN COLEBY – 'Toffee, roasted nuts – I love candied peel so added loads to mine. I made a giant one for me too as I thought they were great.'

SIMON EBBS – 'Amazingly professional-looking little biscuits that I took to our friends who'd invited us to dinner.'

TIP

FOR A SALTED CARAMEL NUT MOUTHFUL, OMIT THE FRUIT AND USE A COMBINATION OF SALTED ROASTED NUTS AND WHITE CHOCOLATE.

RICCIARELLI

PREPARATION	COOKING	MAKES	VEGETARIAN	DAIRY-FREE	GLUTEN-FREE
10 mins + freezing	12–15 mins	20–30 bite-sized biscuits			

Originally from Tuscany, Italy, this is a truly lovely little mouthful, somewhere between a lump of cooked marzipan (almond paste) and a macaroon. Ricciarelli traditionally contain candied peel and are eaten at Christmas, but I don't use the peel and serve them all year. I like the addition of vanilla and, sometimes, I add a few toasted fennel or caraway seeds for a really continental taste. I love to dip mine into a sticky liqueur but they are often served with sweet dessert wine or a really good espresso.

1 egg white
150 g (5 oz/1½ cups) ground almonds
100 g (3½ oz/generous ¾ cup) icing (confectioners') sugar, sifted, plus extra for dusting
5 g (¼ oz) vanilla extract

1. Whisk the egg white until stiff in a clean bowl.
2. Add the rest of the ingredients and mix well – do not worry about folding in or retaining the air from the egg white.
3. Cover the mixture in the bowl with cling film (plastic wrap) and put the mixture into the freezer for 1 hour (or leave in the fridge overnight). It needs chilling before it can be rolled.
4. Preheat the oven to 190°C (375°F/Gas 5).
5. When thoroughly chilled, dust a work surface with a little icing sugar and use your hands to roll the mixture into a 3 cm (1¼ in) diameter log. Flatten the log slightly, then dust the top with icing sugar. Cut it into 1 cm (½ in) pieces and place on a baking sheet covered in baking paper.
6. Bake for 12–15 minutes or until risen and slightly browned. Cool on a wire rack and store in an airtight container for up to 1 month.

WHAT THE TESTERS SAY

BEN COLEBY – 'I added fennel seeds and served them with a sticky liqueur – would also be great with a small coffee after dinner.'

DI PALUMBO – 'I added lemon zest to the recipe and offered them to friends after dinner with a glass of limoncello – and, of course, a little espresso – I am half Italian!'

JOVANKA BJELIC – 'I love these – they are small but really satisfying, so I save them in a little tin just for me and have 1 or 2 when I need something sweet.'

TIP
FOR A CHRISTMAS TREAT, HALF-DIP THESE INTO SOME VERY DARK, MELTED CHOCOLATE.

Opposite: clockwise from the top: Sour Cherry Mini Florentines; Snowball Truffles; Ricciarelli; Leftover Cake Truffles

LEFTOVER CAKE TRUFFLES

| **PREPARATION** 15 mins + chilling | **CHILL-TIME** 1 hour | **MAKES** about 20 truffles | **VEGETARIAN** | **NUT-FREE** |

WHAT THE TESTERS SAY

I like leftovers and view them more as readymade ingredients rather than something to try and use up. Here we use a fabulous-tasting, ready-prepared cake just perfect for truffles. Freeze leftover bits of any flavoured cake and keep them ready to make a batch of these lovely truffles. You can simply roll the truffles in cocoa powder rather than dipping in chocolate if you prefer. Try white chocolate in place of dark or milk chocolate.

PENNY VICKERS – 'I never have leftover cake so I had to put a slice aside for this. I froze them and got them out when we had friends for dinner.'

LYDIA CUFFLIN AND SIMON CHILDS – 'Using leftover cake seems like you are getting something extra for nothing – we've made these in our chalet with ginger cake, fruit cake, plain sponge and even with an open packet of plain biscuits.'

130 g (4½ oz) dark or milk chocolate
20 g (¾ oz) clear honey or golden (corn) syrup
120 g (4 oz) leftover cake
dash of liqueur, or a few drops of vanilla extract or other flavouring (optional)

MARGARET LEE – 'Having leftover cake was a bit of a problem as my husband, Ken, usually eats his way through the lot, down to the last crumb. However, I saved a bit of Madeira cake and made the truffles (to go with the snowballs) for after-dinner coffee when entertaining friends.'

1. Melt 30 g (1 oz) of the chocolate with the honey in a bowl over a pan of boiling water. Remove from the heat.
2. Crumb the leftover cake into the bowl, using your fingers or a hand blender, and add to the chocolate.
3. Add the liqueur or other flavouring, if using, and with wet hands roll the mixture into small bite-sized balls. Freeze for 1 hour to firm.
4. Meanwhile, melt the remaining chocolate in a clean bowl over the pan of water and, using a fork, lift the frozen truffles down into the chocolate and lift out onto a plate lined with baking paper.
5. Store in an airtight container in the fridge for up to 2 weeks.

SNOWBALL TRUFFLES

PREPARATION	CHILL-TIME	MAKES	VEGETARIAN	GLUTEN-FREE	NUT-FREE
10 mins + chilling	4 hours	about 24 truffles			

We are always looking for wintery and snowy treats for the chalets and here is a truffle perfect for winter and Christmas time. They are ridiculously easy – leave them in the freezer until you need them. They are, of course, incredibly sweet but that's exactly why they're a treat and not something you'd devour every day.

115 g (4 oz) white chocolate
100 g (3½ oz) desiccated coconut
100 g (3½ oz) full-fat cream cheese
70 g (2½ oz/generous ½ cup) icing (confectioners') sugar
extra desiccated coconut, for coating

1. Melt the white chocolate in a bowl over a pan of boiling water or on a low setting in the microwave.
2. Add the rest of the ingredients and mix together. Chill slightly if needed and, using wet hands, roll into little balls (these are rich, so smaller is better).
3. Roll the little snowballs in extra desiccated coconut to coat completely.
4. Chill for at least 4 hours then store in the fridge, or freeze and only remove about 20 minutes before serving.

WHAT THE TESTERS SAY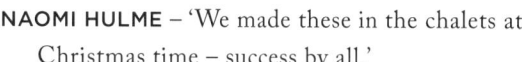

NAOMI HULME – 'We made these in the chalets at Christmas time – success by all.'

CATHERINE AND MATTHEW SELLS – 'We all loved these snowballs (particularly licking the bowl and spoon) and they'll be joining the peppermint creams in gift boxes for Christmas.'

MARGARET LEE – 'It really is lovely to spoil friends with homemade treats and these brilliant little snowballs finished off the meal perfectly. Enjoyed by everyone – even those who thought they were too full!'

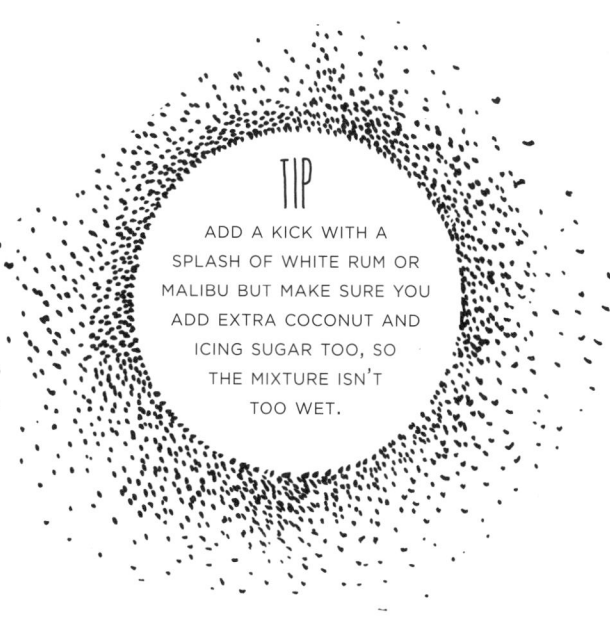

TIP
ADD A KICK WITH A SPLASH OF WHITE RUM OR MALIBU BUT MAKE SURE YOU ADD EXTRA COCONUT AND ICING SUGAR TOO, SO THE MIXTURE ISN'T TOO WET.

'NO-COOK' COCONUT ICE

PREPARATION 5 mins | **COOKING** none | **MAKES** 20–30 squares | **VEGETARIAN** | **GLUTEN-FREE**

The other Lucy has been a constant fan of coconut ice ever since I have known her. When she suggested it for the book I have to say it was not top of my list, but then she arrived at one of our catering functions with a batch she had just made and my mind was absolutely turned around. It was our usual crowd of backroom staff in the kitchen – that is 'women of a certain age' (ourselves included) – and everyone went 'Ooh, takes me back to my childhood!' on eating her crumbly, pink and white confection. This is most definitely 'retro', but comfortingly so.

250 g (9 oz) sweetened condensed milk
250 g (9 oz/2 cups) icing (confectioners') sugar, sifted, plus extra for dusting
200 g (7 oz/2¼ cups) desiccated coconut
a few drops of pink food colouring
pinch of freeze-dried raspberry powder (optional)

1. Using a wooden spoon, mix together the condensed milk and icing sugar in a large bowl. Work the coconut into the mix until it's well combined – you may have to get messy and use your hands.
2. Remove half of the mix and put it to one side and then add a few drops of food colouring and the freeze-dried raspberry, if using, to the remainder in the bowl.
3. Dust a clean work surface with icing sugar, then shape each half into a smooth rectangle about 1 cm (½ in) thick. Put a sheet of baking paper on a small chopping board and transfer the coconut ice to the board, placing one rectangle on top of the other. Press the top of the coconut ice lightly with the flat of your hand to bond the 2 layers.
4. Cover loosely with paper towels and leave for at least 3 hours or overnight to set and dry out slightly.
5. Cut into squares with a sharp knife (a serrated bread or ham knife is best) and pack into airtight jars or sealed bags. It will keep for up to a month.

WHAT THE TESTERS SAY

CLAIRE VAN DIJK – 'Coconut is one of my favourite foods. Lucy LT brought this to a catering function and I went home and made it the next day. Maybe it is a girl thing, because my mum and sister loved it but my husband and son did not.'

PENNY VICKERS – 'Memories of being young – I made it for a group of friends and we spent the whole evening talking about when we were at school.'

JOVANKA BJELIC – 'I loved this when I was small! I included the freeze-dried raspberries and thought they were a great addition. I gave them to friends and family.'

TIP
BE PREPARED TO GET A BIT STICKY AND MESSY WITH THIS ONE – IT'S HANDS-ON!

from left to right: Coconut Ice; Peppermint Creams

PEPPERMINT CREAMS

PREPARATION	COOKING	MAKES	VEGETARIAN	NUT-FREE	DAIRY-FREE	GLUTEN-FREE
10 mins	none	about 30 creAms				

Peppermint creams are a welcome blast from the past. The other Lucy loves these but not as much as she loves them when she makes them with violet essence in place of peppermint for a delightful retro after-dinner treat. Try making them with other flavours and colours – orange, lemon, rose, violet – and cutting into different shapes. Always use natural flavourings and add just enough for a good taste. Use the tip of a skewer or cocktail stick to add the food colouring (to ensure you don't overdo it).

1 egg white
a few drops of peppermint extract
350 g (12 oz/scant 3 cups) icing (confectioners') sugar plus extra for rolling out
food colouring (optional)

1. Lightly whisk the egg white for 4–5 seconds to break it down a little and make it runny.
2. Add a few drops of peppermint extract and whisk in.
3. Sift in the icing sugar and mix to a stiff paste. It needs to be dry enough to hold its shape when rolled out and cut into shapes. Taste to check if you need to add more flavouring.
4. If colouring, divide the paste into 2 and add enough green food colouring to give a nice minty colour to one half.
5. Cover any peppermint cream mixture you are not immediately rolling out with cling film (plastic wrap) to prevent it getting dry. Dust the work surface with sifted icing sugar and roll out the paste to 7–8 mm thick. Cut into 4 cm (1½ in) rounds using a small pastry cutter, dipping the edge of the cutter into icing sugar to help prevent it sticking. (If you haven't got the correct-sized cutter, use something else, such as an egg cup.)
6. Transfer the peppermint creams to baking paper and cover with a clean tea towel to dry out.
7. When dry, store in an airtight container layered with baking paper for up to 4 weeks.

ALTERNATIVE

CHOCOLATE PEPPERMINT CREAMS – Make the peppermint creams (or other flavoured ones) in the usual way and leave to set. Drop ½-teaspoon blobs of melted dark chocolate well apart onto baking paper on a baking sheet. Gently press the dried creams onto the chocolate, then leave to set.

WHAT THE THE TESTERS SAY

CLAIRE VAN DIJK – 'I made these into small, round, very pepperminty balls, dipped them in very dark chocolate and served them as an after-dinner sweet.'

TOM ROBERTS – 'A great dairy-free treat and ridiculously easy to make.'

CATHERINE AND MATTHEW SELLS – 'Matthew and his friends from up the road were confined to the house in bad weather but had great fun making these peppermint creams. We'll be doing them again for Christmas gifts and will go mad decorating with sugar balls, sprinkles and chocolate.'

HONEYCOMB

PREPARATION	COOKING	MAKES	VEGETARIAN	GLUTEN-FREE	NUT-FREE	DAIRY-FREE
5 mins	about 10 mins	about 300 g (10½ oz) honeycomb				

This is fun, a bit like doing a chemistry experiment in your kitchen! It is an instant hit and you can smother it in chocolate or add a few extra flavours, such as a few fennel seeds, chopped nuts or caraway seeds to the boiling syrup. It is simply brilliant for older children to make, exciting for younger children to be a part of making and it is not just for eating on its own as a treat. Try crumbling it and sprinkling it over cake icing, using it on ice cream, or serving chunks alongside a mousse.

120 g (4 oz) golden (corn) syrup or local honey
200 g (7 oz/scant 1 cup) caster (superfine) sugar
15 g (½ oz) bicarbonate of soda (baking soda)

1 Line a 20 cm (8 in) square baking tin with baking paper.
2 Slowly melt the honey and sugar together in a large heavy-based saucepan over a low heat – do not do this over a medium or high heat or the sugar will crystallise and never dissolve. This will take about 5 minutes. Stir from time to time. Then turn up the heat and allow the mix to boil rapidly. Stir occasionally and watch and smell as it starts to turn from golden to dark golden to brown – catch it somewhere between dark golden and dark brown. Get ready, this is the exciting bit now.
3 Throw in the bicarbonate of soda and stir quickly – the mixture will bubble up madly.
4 Pour straight into the tin and leave it to cool and set – it will carry on bubbling a little, then set containing the bubbles. Allow it to go completely cold.
5 Break it into chunks for eating.

WHAT THE TESTERS SAY

HATTIE CUFFLIN – 'First time made and a success! I covered mine in a thick layer of chocolate.'

LYNSEY JONES AND HELEN WOOLDRIDGE – 'We loved making this and just could not wait to smother it in chocolate.'

MICHAEL CUFFLIN (AGED 13) – 'This was like a chemistry experiment – I couldn't believe the way it frothed up. We dipped it in warm, melted chocolate and ate it like a fondue.'

TIP
YOU NEED TO ALLOW THE SUGAR SYRUP MIXTURE TO TURN TO A DARK CARAMEL AS IT WILL NOT SET SOLIDLY IF NOT – AND IT NEEDS THE SLIGHTLY BITTER FLAVOUR TO WORK.

What's the difference between a traybake and a cake? In my head a cake is deep and cut in large slices but a traybake is something slimmer and works well cut into squares, bars or triangles. I also think that a traybake is something be eaten with fingers – and not needing a plate and fork.

In this chapter there are traybakes for all palates – some super-sweet and colourful aimed at younger tastebuds but there are other, rather grown-up, flavours that just happen to work well in a tray.

A quick tip for this chapter – you need to use the right sized tin for the recipes. Many use a 20 cm (8 in) square tin – you can use a cake tin or a shallower baking/roasting tin but if you use a tin larger than the recipe states, the bake will be thinner than intended and won't have the right texture or consistency once cooked. Before you get baking, check out my general tips on page 8 – enjoy!

TRAYBAKES

DAIM AND WHITE CHOCOLATE TRAYBAKE

PREPARATION 15 mins | **COOKING** 20–25 mins | **MAKES** 16 bars | **VEGETARIAN**

I worked in Sweden for a year in the 80s – that was before the UK had its own Ikea and most Brits had not tasted a Daim bar. I bought one on my first Ikea experience in Stockholm and have been in love with them ever since. You'll see I have several recipes that include them in this book – such is my penchant for them. You can use any chocolate chunks if you have no Daim. A word of warning – this recipe is super-sweet and sickly!

60 g (2 oz) butter, at room temperature
125 g (4 oz/generous ½ cup) caster (superfine) sugar
1 egg
5 g (¼ oz) vanilla extract
175 g (6 oz/scant 1½ cups) self-raising flour
4 x 28 g (1 oz) Daim bars, chopped
250 g (9 oz) white chocolate, chopped
125 g (4 oz) mascarpone cheese

1. Preheat the oven to 180°C (350°F/Gas 4). Line a 20 cm (8 in) square baking tin with baking paper.
2. Beat the butter and sugar together in a mixing bowl until creamy, then add the egg and vanilla and beat well.
3. Add the flour and stir in with 2 of the chopped Daim bars. Mix well and press into the lined tin. Use a spatula to get all the mix out of the bowl then you can use the bowl for the topping without washing it.
4. Bake for 20–25 minutes or until golden on the top. Remove from the oven and allow it to get completely cold in the tin.
5. Put the white chocolate into the same mixing bowl and place it over a pan of boiling water until melted. Remove the bowl from the pan and allow to cool for 5 minutes (this is important).
6. Beat in the mascarpone cheese. It will become a thick, white goo. Spread this over the cold base and scatter the rest of the Daim bars over. Chill in the fridge to set before cutting into squares. Store in an airtight container for a week or two.

WHAT THE TESTERS SAY

KERRY GREGORY – 'If you love Daims you will love these. They are a great treat. I might try it with very dark chocolate chips in place of the Daim next time.'

SARITA KATTOJU AND ROHIT PABLA – 'Gosh these are sweet – good sweet though. We would make them again but as a special treat.'

CLAIRE VAN DIJK – 'A great combo with mascarpone as part of the icing – it makes for a really thick topping. I also made a batch using milk chocolate instead of white, which also worked well, but the Daim bar did not show up so much on the top.'

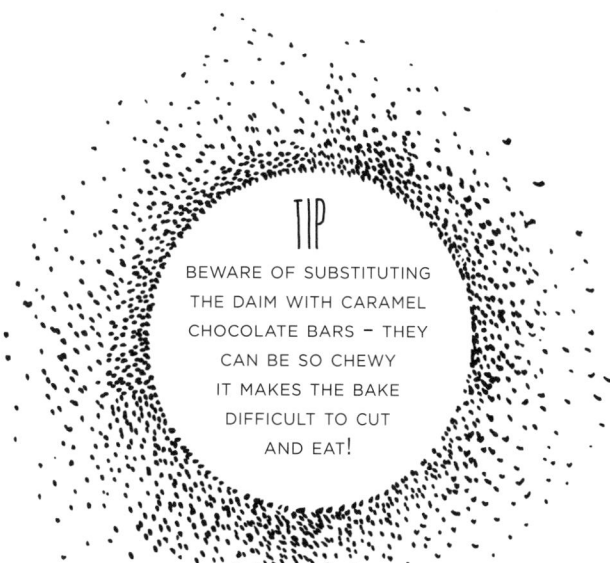

TIP
BEWARE OF SUBSTITUTING THE DAIM WITH CARAMEL CHOCOLATE BARS – THEY CAN BE SO CHEWY IT MAKES THE BAKE DIFFICULT TO CUT AND EAT!

SAM'S EASTER ROCKY ROAD

| PREPARATION | COOKING | MAKES | VEGETARIAN | GLUTEN-FREE |
| 15 mins | none (except melting) | 15 bars | | |

Sam, my son, is now 18 and a master of rocky road as he has made it since he was very small. He makes many flavours but this is one of his favourites and a great alternative to giving an Easter egg (pack them into little cellophane bags or boxes). There is little more to say other than you can, of course, make this in many flavours at any time of year (see my alternatives opposite) but whatever flavour you choose there is no doubt that Sam's recipe is sweet and rich and decadent – enjoy! You can store them in the fridge for up to 2 weeks or freeze them for up to 2 months.

125 g (4 oz) butter
250 g (9 oz) milk chocolate
30 g (1 oz) golden (corn) syrup
150 g (5 oz) rich tea biscuits
100 g (3½ oz) mini marshmallows
200 g (7 oz) chocolate mini eggs

1 Line a 20 cm (8 in) square baking tin with a double layer of cling film (plastic wrap).
2 Melt the butter, chocolate and syrup in a large saucepan, stirring all the time, then remove from the heat.
3 Put the biscuits into a strong plastic bag and crush them roughly with a rolling pin. You want to see the bits, so don't over-crush.
4 Wait for 8–10 minutes while the chocolate mixture cools then add the biscuits, marshmallows and half the eggs.
5 Spoon it into the tin, place the eggs evenly over the top and press it all down together, shoving the eggs into the mixture as you do.
6 Chill in the fridge for at least 2 hours before cutting into squares.

ALTERNATIVES

Omit the chocolate mini eggs and add instead:
TURKISH DELIGHT – 2 x 51 g (2 oz) bars chocolate Turkish delight, chopped.
FUDGE AND MALTESER – 1 x 25 g (1 oz) chocolate fudge bar, chopped, and 3 x 37g (1½ oz) packets of Maltesers.
PINK CRANBERRY – use pink marshmallows instead of white and add 100 g (3½ oz) dried cranberries.
JELLY BEANS – 200 g (7 oz) jelly beans.
HONEYCOMB – 2 x 40 g (1½ oz) Crunchie bars (or homemade see page 100), roughly chopped.

WHAT THE TESTERS SAY

KERRY GREGORY – 'A great family bake as it was really easy for the children to make. We ate it for Sunday afternoon tea and kept it chilled in the fridge to enjoy during the week. I may have a go with dark chocolate next time.'

JANE BOLTON – 'These are sweet and we really enjoyed getting messy in the kitchen with the children. We used M&Ms.'

SARITA KATTOJU AND ROHIT PABLA – 'A hit with us. Wrong time of year for easter eggs so used Maltesers – fantastic!'

Opposite: top, Sam's Easter Rocky Road; middle, Key Lime Bars; bottom, Specaloo Tiffin

KEY LIME BARS

PREPARATION 10 mins | **COOKING** 25 mins | **MAKES** 16 squares or 15 bars | **VEGETARIAN**

Key lime pie is an American dessert with a biscuit base and a mousse top made with condensed milk and limes. Here is a traybake using similar ingredients. Condensed milk is an unusual baking ingredient and gives cakes and biscuits a chewier texture. This mixture is quite solid, which makes it ideal for a traybake to be cut into bars to eat. See the finished bake on page 107.

FOR THE BARS
175 g (6 oz) butter, at room temperature
75 g (2½ oz/⅓ cup) caster (superfine) sugar
250 g (9 oz) sweetened condensed milk
finely grated zest and juice of 2 limes
3 eggs
200 g (7 oz/1⅔ cups) self-raising flour

FOR THE DRIZZLE
100 g (3½ oz) icing (confectioners') sugar, sifted
finely grated zest and juice of 2 limes

FOR THE FROSTING
100 g (3½ oz) full-fat cream cheese
250 g (9 oz/generous 1 cup) icing (confectioners') sugar, sifted
75 g (2½ oz) butter, at room temperature
finely grated zest of 1 lime

1. Preheat the oven to 180°C (350°F/Gas 4). Line a 20 cm (8 in) square baking tin with baking paper.
2. Beat the butter and sugar together in a bowl using a wooden spoon or an electric whisk. Add the condensed milk, lime zest and juice and mix well. Add the eggs, then the flour and mix until well combined.
3. Turn into the prepared tin and bake for 25 minutes or until the centre springs back when lightly pressed.
4. Meanwhile, make the drizzle. Mix the icing sugar, lime zest and juice together and thin, if necessary, with a little water to make a thin drizzle. When the cake is cooked but still hot in the tin, spoon it over and leave it to soak in.
5. Make the frosting. Beat the cream cheese, icing sugar and butter together to make the frosting and spread over the cake when cold, topping with the grated lime zest, then cut into bars. Store in an airtight container.

WHAT THE TESTERS SAY

MARCELLA SCOTT – 'I made this in a smaller cake tin – it worked really well as a deep cake, super easy, super tasty.'

NAOMI HULME – 'Super easy! Make sure you have the right sized tin or they would be very deep, but a great flavour.'

PENNY VICKERS – 'I had these as a pudding with my husband and rugby-trainee lodger. I used gluten-free flour and they worked a treat – sweet and really zingy.'

> **TIP**
> TO GET MAXIMUM JUICE FROM YOUR LIMES, POP THEM IN THE MICROWAVE FOR 30 SECONDS BEFORE SQUEEZING.

SPECALOO TIFFIN

PREPARATION	COOKING	MAKES	VEGETARIAN
15 mins + chilling	none (except melting)	12 bars	

Specaloo biscuits are from Belgium. They are crispy, plain biscuits with a dark caramel flavour. You may have come across them, individually wrapped, with a coffee in a hairdressers or coffee bar and you can buy them in packets in the supermarkets called by their brand name 'Lotus biscuits'. They turn this tiffin into something just a bit more special. I like this married with a thick layer of dark chocolate on the top, but you could use milk or white chocolate if you prefer. See the finished bake on page 107.

250 g (9 oz) specaloo biscuits
150 g (5 oz) butter
40 g (1½ oz/⅓ cup) cocoa powder
50 g (2 oz/¼ cup) caster (superfine) sugar
80 g (3 oz) golden (corn) syrup
50 g (2 oz/½ cup) raisins
50 g (2 oz/½ cup) pecan nuts, roughly chopped
200 g (7 oz) milk or dark chocolate

1. Line a 20 cm (8 in) square baking tin with a double layer of cling film (plastic wrap).
2. Put the biscuits into a strong plastic bag and crush them thoroughly with a rolling pin.
3. Melt the butter, cocoa, sugar and syrup in a large saucepan, stirring all the time.
4. Add the biscuits, raisins and nuts to the melted mixture, stir well and press into the lined tin.
5. Chill for 1 hour in the fridge. Break up the chocolate and place in a bowl over a pan of boiling water and stir occasionally until melted. Spread it over the top of the cooled tiffin. Leave to set.
6. Cut into bars to serve. Store in an airtight container for a week or two.

WHAT THE TESTERS SAY

NAOMI HULME – 'They would be nice with any variety of dried fruits or chopped stem ginger and cut really small they'd make great petit fours.'

JOVANKA BJELIC – 'Brilliant recipe – I struggled to get the biscuits at first but you could use other types. I shared them in the staff room at school – plate empty in minutes.'

JANE BOLTON – 'I think this would be good with dark chocolate and although I liked the specaloos, we did them again with digestives and we liked those too – great tiffin recipe.'

TIP
IF YOU CANNOT GET LOTUS BISCUITS, TRY GINGER NUTS OR USE THE MORE USUAL DIGESTIVES (GRAHAM CRACKERS).

PEANUT BUTTER CRISPY SQUARES

PREPARATION	COOKING	MAKES	VEGETARIAN	GLUTEN-FREE	NUT-FREE
10 mins	none (except melting)	16			

Sam, my son, has been a peanut butter fan since he was little. When we first cooked together we used to make chocolate crispies and marshmallow crispies, but it was his idea to add the peanuts – only we had none so we added peanut butter – a few tweaks later we had a recipe. It is so easy it is hardly a recipe at all. A great thing to make with small children.

40 g (1½ oz) butter
250 g (9 oz) marshmallows
200 g (9 oz) peanut butter
250 g (9 oz) puffed rice cereal
50 g (2 oz/⅓ cup) salted peanuts, chopped

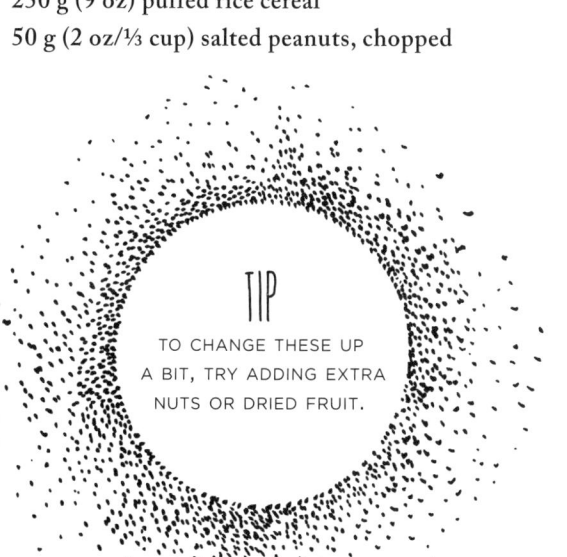

TIP
TO CHANGE THESE UP A BIT, TRY ADDING EXTRA NUTS OR DRIED FRUIT.

1 Line a 20 cm (8 in) square baking tin with a double layer of cling film (plastic wrap).
2 Melt the butter, marshmallows and peanut butter together in a large saucepan, stirring.
3 Add the cereal and peanuts and thoroughly mix together so they are totally covered in the marshmallow mix.
4 Press into the prepared tin and chill until set. Cut into squares. Store in an airtight container for up to a week or so.

WHAT THE TESTERS SAY

KERRY GREGORY – 'These are very, very easy and very, very tasty.'

JOVANKA BJELIC – 'Oh my goodness – they did not last long in our house.'

SARITA KATTOJU AND ROHIT PABLA – 'Rohit made these with me – so simple and we both agreed a great treat to keep in the biscuit tin!'

PARSNIP AND GINGER TRAYBAKE

PREPARATION	COOKING	MAKES	VEGETARIAN	NUT-FREE
15 mins	30–35 mins	12 squares		

I am always looking for great flavour combinations and I think that the parsnip and ginger here is a real winner, made that bit more interesting with the addition of a little coconut. Make sure you weigh the parsnip after grating and use the fine side of the grater. If the pieces are too large, they won't cook in time. The honey buttercream is to die for!

FOR THE CAKE

200 g (7 oz/1⅔ cups) plain (all-purpose) flour
10 g (½ oz) baking powder
125 g (4 oz) plain yoghurt
120 g (4 oz/½ cup) caster (superfine) sugar
75 g (2½ oz/generous ¾ cup) desiccated coconut
2 eggs
175 g (6 oz) grated parsnip
10 g (½ oz) ground ginger
120 g (4 oz) butter, melted
50 g (2 oz) clear honey

FOR THE BUTTERCREAM

150 g (5 oz) butter, at room temperature
200 g (7 oz/1⅔ cups) icing (confectioners') sugar, sifted
50 g (2 oz) clear honey
a little crystallised ginger, chopped, to decorate

1. Preheat the oven to 180°C (350°F/Gas 4). Line a 20 cm (8 in) square baking tin with baking paper.
2. Put all the cake ingredients into a mixing bowl and mix with a wooden spoon or a hand whisk until well blended.
3. Transfer the mixture to the prepared tin and bake for 30–35 minutes or until risen, browned and springy to the touch.
4. Allow to cool in the tin as this is a moist cake.
5. Meanwhile, make the buttercream. Mix the butter and icing sugar together until smooth then add the honey a little at a time or it will curdle, beating well after each addition. Spread or pipe the buttercream over the cake when it is completely cold then scatter the top with a little chopped crystallised ginger.
6. Cut into squares to serve. Store the remainder in an airtight container for up to a week or so.

WHAT THE TESTERS SAY

HELEN WOOLDRIDGE AND LYNSEY JONES – 'An unusual sounding cake that got our chalet guests talking and they were very pleasantly surprised on tasting it. The honey butter icing was lovely, subtle and different but went with the other flavours really well.'

FI GALLAGHER AND OLLIE EVANS – 'Our favourite – we love unusual-sounding cakes but even though the idea seemed new, the overall tastes were clean and classic.'

CLAIRE VAN DIJK – 'I have made this many times now and it works every time – the honey buttercream is a triumph and I use it on other cakes, especially a lemon cake.'

TIP

Although I've included this as a traybake, you can also cook it in a 20 cm (8 in) round cake tin or, even two sandwich tins and sandwich it together with the buttercream.

FLORENTINE BARS

PREPARATION	COOKING	MAKES	VEGETARIAN
15 mins + cooling	35–40 mins	16 bars	

On Saturday mornings when I was small my father walked me, my brothers and sister to my granny's house via a continental bakery (very unusual for those days – the bakery not the walk!). My father would choose a coffee éclair, my brother a lemon bun, but I would choose a giant Florentine – all those nuts and toffee stuck to a thick slab of very dark chocolate. Perhaps an odd choice for a 5-year-old but I loved them all the same. I have grown to realise that this intense combination is not everyone's cup of tea, so this is a version of a Florentine for those with a sweeter tooth – a brown sugar shortbread topped with caramel, nuts and fruit and then a choice of your favourite chocolate to top it all off. This recipe works very well with any combination of fruit and nut.

FOR THE BASE
150 g (5 oz) butter
75 g (2½ oz/⅓ cup) demerara (raw) sugar
250 g (9 oz/2 cups) self-raising flour

FOR THE TOPPING
5 g (2½ oz) butter, at room temperature
150 g (5 oz/generous ⅔ cup) demerara (raw) sugar
1 large egg
70 g (2½ oz) golden (corn) syrup
100 g (3½ oz/generous ½ cup) dried apricots, chopped or cranberries
100 g (3½ oz/¾ cup) whole hazelnuts or pistachios
100 g (3½ oz) dark chocolate, melted

1. Preheat the oven to 180°C (350°F/Gas 4). Line a 20 cm (8 in) square baking tin with baking paper.
2. Rub the butter and sugar into the flour to make the base using your fingers and thumbs. It may still be crumbly, but squeeze it together a little and let the warmth of your hands bring it together, then press it into the base of the tin. Set the bowl aside to make the topping in.
3. Bake for 20 minutes or until it is golden in colour. Allow it to cool for 10 minutes.
4. Meanwhile make the topping. Beat the butter and sugar in the bowl until mixed, then beat in the egg. Add the remaining topping ingredients except the chocolate and spread over the slightly cooled shortbread. Return this to the oven for a further 15–20 minutes or until it is golden brown all over.
5. Remove from the oven and leave until completely cold in the tin. Break up the chocolate and place in a bowl over a pan of boiling water and stir occasionally until melted. Drizzle the traybake with the melted chocolate. When the chocolate has set, cut into triangles or squares.

WHAT THE THE TESTERS SAY

DI PALUMBO – 'I never think I am going to like a traybake as I assume they will be too sweet but these were fabulous. I used 70 per cent chocolate for extra bitterness and might add some ginger next time.'

LIZ EVERSON – 'I made a family-friendly version of these with almonds and sour cherries, topped with milk chocolate – they did not last long in the tin.'

BEN COLEBY – 'I thought these were really delicious. I made the mini Florentines (see page 90) and then these as an alternative – I liked both but these were more of a teatime biscuit.'

ALMOND BLONDIES

PREPARATION	COOKING	MAKES	VEGETARIAN
10 mins	25–30 mins	16 squares	

I feel very privileged to have worked with Skiworld for many years as it has given me reasons to explore the local cuisines of France, Austria, Switzerland and North America. In fact, I would probably not have made the effort to find these delightful traybakes if I had not been searching for new recipes for the chalets in the Rockies. Of course, blondies are not new but, being white chocolate-based, they are a pleasant change from chocolate brownies. Originally made with macadamia nuts in our chalets, I think the almonds are better as they have better flavour once baked. So thanks Skiworld for this one!

60 g (2 oz) butter, at room temperature
125 g (4 oz/generous ½ cup) demerara (raw) sugar
1 egg
15 g (½ oz) vanilla extract
125 g (4 oz/1 cup) plain (all-purpose) flour
50 g (2 oz/½ cup) ground almonds
5 g (1/4 oz) baking powder
3 g (⅛ oz) salt
100 g (3½ oz) white chocolate, chopped
100 g (3½ oz/⅔ cup) whole almonds, roughly chopped

TIP
YOU CAN ALWAYS REVERT TO MACADAMIA NUTS IF YOU WISH OR TRY USING SALTED, ROASTED PEANUTS IN PLACE OF ALMONDS AND USE HALF THE SALT.

1. Preheat the oven to 180°C (350°F/Gas 4). Line a 20 cm (8 in) square baking tin with baking paper.
2. Cream the butter and sugar together in a mixing bowl using a wooden spoon or an electric whisk.
3. Add the egg and vanilla extract and beat well.
4. Fold in the dry ingredients except the nuts using a metal spoon.
5. Transfer the mixture to the prepared baking tin and level with a spatula. Sprinkle with the chopped whole almonds and press slightly into the batter. Bake for 25–30 minutes.
6. Cool in the tin and then cut into squares.

WHAT THE TESTERS SAY

HELEN WOOLDRIDGE AND LYNSEY JONES – 'We had no whole almonds so used walnuts – more grown-up flavour but great all the same and we served them as a pud with ice cream and berries.'

MANDY FISHER – 'I made them for the hubby and I wouldn't make any changes to them apart from drizzling with melted white chocolate!'

KAJAL MISTRY – 'An easy-to-follow recipe and I loved the flavour. I thought the vanilla would be too much but not at all and the almonds were really good in them. I used a larger tin, so mine were a bit flatter than the picture and looked and tasted like giant square cookies.'

Opposite: front, Peanut Butter Jelly Bars; middle, Lottie's Loaded Bites; back, Almond Blondies

PEANUT BUTTER JELLY BARS

PREPARATION	COOKING	MAKES	VEGETARIAN
15 mins	30 mins	12 bars	

We Brits would, of course, say peanut butter and jam but I think the American word jelly sounds more fun! The saltiness and nuttiness of the peanuts and the sweet sharpness of the jam are a match made in heaven and one that works here perfectly in these moreish morsels. They are great as part of a packed lunch or a snack-pack for a long walk. See the finished bake on page 117.

125 g (4 oz) butter, at room temperature
150 g (5 oz/⅔ cup) caster (superfine) sugar
250 g (9 oz) smooth peanut butter
1 egg
5 g (¼ oz) vanilla extract
180 g (6 oz/1½ cups) plain (all-purpose) flour, sifted
5 g (¼ oz) baking powder
about ⅓ x 340 g (12 oz) jar raspberry jam (jelly) or other jam (or see my recipe on page 192)
50 g (2 oz/⅓ cup) salted peanuts, coarsely chopped

1   Preheat the oven to 190°C (375°F/Gas 5). Line a 20 x 20 cm (8 x 10 in) baking tin with baking paper.
2   Beat the butter and sugar together in a bowl using a wooden spoon or an electric whisk. Add the peanut butter and mix well.
3   Add the egg, vanilla, flour and baking powder and beat to a stiff dough.
4   Press two-thirds of the mixture into the prepared tin and then spread a thick layer of jam over. Don't skimp on the jam here.
5   Dot the rest of the mixture over the top of the jam in clumps using your hands and scatter over the chopped peanuts.
6   Bake for 30 minutes or until dark golden brown and slightly risen.
7   Allow to cool in the tin and then cut into bars. Store in an airtight container for a week or two.

WHAT THE TESTERS SAY

SAMUEL RAFTER – 'I like these best with raspberry jam and I added more as I like the jam to be a thick layer. I love peanuts and peanut butter, so these are one of my favourites.'

IAN COLEBY – 'Lucy made these for me for my bike rides as they are a perfect salt and sweet combo, so I tried to make them myself and even as a complete novice baker I was utterly surprised I could make something like this. I used blackcurrant jam.'

ANNETTE MEEKCOMS – 'I made these while we were on holiday in the mountains. We all loved them and they were eaten as soon as the hordes came in from skiing.'

TIP
TRY REDCURRANT JELLY IN PLACE OF JAM FOR A SHARPER CONTRAST.

LOTTIE'S LOADED BITES

PREPARATION	COOKING	MAKES	VEGETARIAN
10 mins	25 mins	12 bars	

My friend Annette (known as Lottie though I know not why) and I were messing about in the kitchen on a bad weather day on holiday. We wondered what would happen if you baked a rocky road mixture (as you do!). We did and it was a confused-tasting mess, but we were not put off and we slightly deconstructed the ingredients and ended up with this utterly scrumptious tray of ultra-sweetness. We called it Lottie's loaded bites because really you can load the topping up as much as you like with almost whatever you like – we tried it with pieces of Bounty bar, Daim bar, sweets and all sorts of nuts – this was our favourite combo. See the finished bake on page 117. Happy baking!

FOR THE BASE
250 g (9 oz) digestive biscuits (graham crackers)
150 g (5 oz) butter

FOR THE TOPPING
120 g (4 oz/¾ cup) salted roasted peanuts
100 g (3½ oz) mini marshmallows
50 g (2 oz) dried sour cherries
250 g (9 oz) sweetened condensed milk
150 g (5 oz) white chocolate, broken in pieces

1. Preheat the oven to 180°C (350°F/Gas 4). Line a 20 cm (8 in) square baking tin with baking paper.
2. Crush the digestive biscuits to a fine crumb in a plastic bag using a rolling pin.
3. Put the butter into a bowl and microwave on full power for 1 minute or until the butter is just melted, or heat gently in a saucepan.
4. Add the biscuit crumbs and stir well. Spoon the mixture into the prepared tin and press down well (it's best to use a metal spoon as it does not stick to the crumb).
5. Chop the peanuts and sprinkle evenly over the base with the marshmallows and cherries – really this is your chance to load these bites up with your favourite things. The marshmallows act as the 'glue' so don't miss these out, but you can have any dried fruit, nuts, chopped chocolate bars and so on.
6. Spoon the condensed milk evenly over the topping and bake for 25 minutes, or until the top is browned.
7. Remove from the oven and allow to cool completely in the tin.
8. Wipe your mixing bowl out and put the white chocolate in. Melt over a pan of boiling water and then drizzle all over the top. Set in the fridge then cut into bars.

WHAT THE TESTERS SAY

IRENE O'SULLIVAN – 'The recipe was super-quick, easy to follow and all made in just one bowl! Everyone in the Skiworld office loved them.'

ANNETTE AND TOBY MEEKCOMS – 'As part-inventors of these we have to admit they are ultra-sweet but we love them. We love them loaded high with salted peanuts, marshmallows and dried cranberries – we also double the chocolate on the top for a really thick layer – mmm!'

HANNAH, AJ AND MADDIE CUFFLIN – 'We loaded ours with buckets of peanuts, pink marshmallows and chocolate chips – really sweet.'

TOFFEE AND APRICOT BREAKFAST BARS

PREPARATION	COOKING	MAKES	VEGETARIAN	NUT-FREE
15 mins	25 mins	18 bars		

I guess I call this a breakfast bar because it sort of contains milk along with being packed with seeds, nuts and oats. There are plenty of good things in these to sustain you through the morning but there is no way these are a low calorie or low-sugar option. They're great as a treat, a snack on the go or as part of a packed lunch. Choose other seeds, such as pumpkin or sesame, use nuts instead, such as chopped hazelnuts or walnuts and different dried fruits. The possibilities are endless!

150 g (5 oz) butter
200 g (7 oz/scant 1 cup) demerara (raw) sugar
50 g (2 oz) golden (corn) syrup
¼ teaspoon instant coffee granules
3 g (⅛ oz) salt
1 x 379 g (14 oz) can sweetened condensed milk
350 g (12 oz/3½ cups) porridge (rolled) oats
200 g (7 oz/generous 1 cup) dried apricots, chopped
150 g (5 oz/1¼ cups) sunflower or other seeds

1. Preheat the oven to 180°C (350°F/Gas 4). Line a 20 x 30 cm (8 x 12 in) shallow baking tin with baking paper.
2. Melt the butter, sugar, syrup, coffee, salt and condensed milk gently together in a large saucepan. Once melted, bring to the boil and boil until the mixture changes colour to light gold, stirring all the time, but do not allow to get too brown.
3. Remove from the heat and stir the remaining ingredients into the mix. Press evenly into the prepared tin.
4. Bake for 25 minutes or until dark golden brown all over.
5. Allow to cool, then cut into bars and remove from the tin. They will keep for up to 2 weeks in an airtight container.

WHAT THE TESTERS SAY

KERRY GREGORY – 'We used raisins instead of apricots but as they are definitely a cereal bar my children were not keen. Perhaps they're more of a grown-up, filling snack bar to pack full of seeds and nuts and put in your pocket.'

PENNY VICKERS – 'I made them for my husband, brother-in-law, two builders, one triathlete and one professional rugby player (who ate it for a post-training snack).'

ROBINSON FAMILY – 'They are sweet but satisfying and I shared them with friends.'

TIP

REDUCE THE OATS SLIGHTLY AND LOAD UP WITH MORE FRUIT AND SEEDS FOR MORE ENERGY.

LUCY'S CHEWY CHOCOLATE BROWNIES

| PREPARATION | COOKING | MAKES | VEGETARIAN | NUT- |
| 10 mins | 20 mins | 12 squares | | FREE |

An American friend of mine told me that she always used cream cheese in her brownies. Sadly I never got her recipe, so this was trial and error. I could not get them to work until I used cocoa in place of chocolate. I also think you get a really big chocolate hit with cocoa. You can add pecans, chocolate chunks, nuts and seeds and this recipe works time and time again. They're delicious as a teatime treat or warm for dessert with some cream or ice cream.

200 g (7 oz) butter
400 g (14 oz/1¾ cups) caster (superfine) sugar
80 g (3 oz/⅔ cup) cocoa powder
4 eggs
5 g (¼ oz) vanilla essence
3 g (⅛ oz) salt
200 g (7 oz) full-fat cream cheese
100 g (3½ oz) self-raising flour
100 g (3½ oz) white chocolate, chopped into small chunks

1. Preheat the oven to 190°C (375°F/Gas 5). Line a 20 x 30 cm (8 x 12 in) shallow baking tin with baking paper.
2. Put the butter and sugar in a large saucepan and gently melt them together over a low heat. Add the cocoa and stir well.
3. Remove from the heat and add the eggs, vanilla, salt and cream cheese, and beat until smooth.
4. Add the flour and fold it in with a metal spoon until just mixed – don't over mix, and don't worry if there are a few lumps.
5. Pour the mixture into the prepared tin and then scatter the chocolate chunks over. Using the handle of the teaspoon, swirl the mixture to spread the chocolate through – just a couple of swirls will do.
6. Bake for 20 minutes until still slightly soft in the centre. Allow them to cool in the tin – they will firm up as they cool.
7. Dust with icing sugar, then cut into squares to serve. Store any remainder in an airtight container in the fridge for up to 3 weeks (remove from the fridge about 15 minutes before eating or they'll be too cold).

WHAT THE TESTERS SAY

ROGER AINGER – 'Never having made cakes before, I could not believe the amount of sinful things that this recipe included. Not for the faint hearted or those on a diet, but having said that, I would make them again. Wicked but good.'

HELEN WOOLDRIDGE AND LYNSEY JONES – 'Don't cook it for longer than it says even if it looks uncooked – when it cools it sets and the stickier the better. Really gooey brownies – great as a teatime treat or warm with ice cream as a pud.'

JO, JOSH AND BEN CURD – 'A real favourite and everyone always asks us for the recipe when we take them anywhere.'

TIP

THE MOST IMPORTANT THING WITH BROWNIES IS NOT TO BE TEMPTED TO OVERCOOK THEM — 20 MINUTES AND THEY ARE DONE — YOU WANT THEM SQUIDGY IN THE MIDDLE WHEN THEY COOL.

HONEY LAVENDER FLAPJACK

PREPARATION 15 mins + cooling | **COOKING** 15–20 mins | **MAKES** 16 bars | **VEGETARIAN** | **GLUTEN-FREE** | **NUT-FREE**

The blend of honey and lavender is quite exceptional. So when your lavender is in flower in the garden, dry a bunch and keep them safe in a jar to try this recipe. I discovered using floral hints in cooking when researching food for a Richard III feast in my hometown of Leicester shortly after his bones were found. I have had lots of fun with flowers since. It is important to use good quality oats (jumbo are great) – the bigger they are the more rustic the flapjack. Very small, cheap oats will give a more cake-like texture.

200 g (7 oz) butter
125 g (4 oz/generous ½ cup) soft light brown or demerara (raw) sugar
100 g (3½ oz) golden (corn) syrup
120 g (4 oz) clear honey
4 heads of dried lavender flowers (1 teaspoon)
300 g (10½ oz/3 cups) porridge (rolled) oats
pinch of salt

1. Preheat the oven to 190°C (375°F/Gas 5). Line a 20 x 25 cm (8 x 10 in) shallow baking tin with baking paper.
2. Melt the butter, sugar, syrup and honey together in a large saucepan.
3. Remove the lavender flowers from the stems, if necessary, and chop them. Add these to the melted mixture with the oats and salt. Mix well and turn it into the tin. Flatten out and bake for 15–20 minutes or until it is a deep golden brown all over and a little caramelised around the edges (if not cooked enough, it won't hold together when cold).
4. Remove from the oven, leave to cool, then cut into squares or bars. Store in an airtight container for several weeks.

WHAT THE TESTERS SAY

CLAIRE VAN DIJK – 'It was me who suggested using lavender to Lucy as I love it in almost any food – so proud it has made the book! I use a lavender honey rather than our local one and add a few poppy seeds for an extra crunch.'

JOVANKA BJELIC – 'I made them just with lavender honey (really delicate flavour). My family did not notice it and just ate them all very quickly. I am now inspired to add unusual flavours to my flapjack, so next I am adding some ground ginger and pieces of crystallised ginger to the mix.'

JACQUI MELVILLE AND SUZANNE QUINTNER – 'We loved this and will be adding lavender to future baking recipes.'

TIP
YOU CAN OF COURSE OMIT THE LAVENDER AND ADD PUMPKIN SEEDS, SOUR CHERRIES, NUTS OR WHATEVER YOU FANCY IF YOU THINK THE FLOWERS ARE A STEP TOO FAR.

LEMON, CORNMEAL AND ROSEMARY TRAY BAKE

PREPARATION 15 mins | **COOKING** 20–25 mins | **MAKES** 12–16 triangles | **VEGETARIAN** | **NUT-FREE**

The other Lucy brought this round to my house one afternoon. She had eaten something like it in Italy (where she seems to do a lot of her eating and tasting!). When she had devoured this deliciously light cake in a café there, she had asked what was in it and they had produced a bag of cornmeal. When she got home, she experimented and transposed a favourite lemon drizzle recipe into this wonderful recipe. The cornmeal makes the cake incredibly light, crumbly and almost a little sandy and its delicate rosemary and lemon flavour make it that bit different from the standard lemon drizzle. It's good as cake or served as a pud with crème fraîche or lightly whipped cream. Fab!

FOR THE CAKE
250 g (9 oz) unsalted butter, at room temperature
250 g (9 oz/generous 1 cup) caster (superfine) sugar
3 eggs
100 g (3½ oz/generous ¾ cup) self-raising flour
3 g (⅛ oz) baking powder
150 g (5 oz/1 cup) fine cornmeal
15 g (½ oz) lemon juice

FOR THE DRIZZLE
finely grated zest and juice of 2 lemons
175 g (6 oz/¾ cup) caster (superfine) sugar
4 g (¼ oz) fresh rosemary, snipped with scissors

1. Preheat the oven to 180°C (350°F/Gas 4). Line a 20 x 30 cm (8 x 12 in) shallow baking tin with baking paper.
2. Using a wooden spoon or electric whisk, beat the butter and sugar until well mixed. Beat in the eggs one at a time, beating well after each addition.
3. Add the flour and baking powder with the cornmeal and lemon juice. Gently fold them all together with a metal spoon.
4. Turn the mixture into the prepared tin, spread out evenly and bake for 20–25 minutes until nicely golden and springy to the touch.
5. Meanwhile make the drizzle. Mix the lemon zest and juice with the sugar and rosemary.
6. As soon as the cake comes out of the oven, drizzle the lemon mixture all over the top, making sure the rosemary is evenly spread. Leave to cool before cutting into squares. Store in an airtight container for up to a week.

WHAT THE TESTERS SAY

SARITA KATTOJU AND ROHIT PABLA (SON) – 'Tangy, aromatic as well as sweet – what's not to love? My friends thought they were fantastic. Serve them warm with crème fraîche as a dessert.'

MARGARET LEE – 'I used fine cornmeal and it was the lightest sponge. I shared it with neighbours and friends who thought the same.'

JACQUI MELVILLE AND SUZANNE QUINTNER – 'We have just made and stolen a corner piece from the tin warm – ooh yummy!'

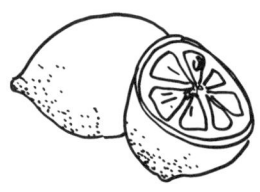

TIP
TRY REPLACING THE ROSEMARY WITH LEMON BALM OR LEMON VERBENA FOR A CHANGE, TOO.

HIGH-ENERGY DATE BARS

| PREPARATION | COOKING | MAKES | VEGAN & | GLUTEN- | DAIRY- |
| 5 mins | none | 12–20 bars | VEGETARIAN | FREE | FREE |

These are pure natural energy – great to have in your pocket on any activity and they last for weeks in the fridge, so make batches with different additions to vary your snacks. You can add extra chopped dried fruit and nuts after you have blended the main mixture to add texture and different flavours. Make then as thick or thin as you like by varying the size of the tin.

200 g (7 oz/1½ cups) nuts of your choice

200 g (7 oz/generous 1 cup) ready-to-eat dried fruit and berries

200 g (7 oz/genereous 1 cup) stoned dates

1. Preheat the oven to 190°C (375°F/Gas 5). Toast the nuts for 5 minutes on a baking sheet then set aside to cool. Line a 20 cm (8 in) square tin with cling film (plastic wrap).
2. Put all the ingredients into a food processor and pulse to mix – it is sticky and you will have to open and re-open the processor to shift the mixture around a bit.
3. Process until the mixture forms a ball.
4. Press the fruit paste into the prepared tin and smooth into an even layer using a non-stick spatula or metal spoon dipped in cold water.
5. Cover with kitchen paper and allow it to dry out over night.
6. Wrap and store in an airtight container in the fridge for several weeks.
7. The bars will freeze well, wrapped individually, so they can be taken out as needed and popped into a backpack ready to head for the great outdoors! (If the bars get a bit warm then they will go to a paste, but still taste great.)

WHAT THE TESTERS SAY

BRENDAN CROFT – 'As a keen cyclist I always ride with a couple of these in my pocket. When they are warm they do lose their shape, but they provide instant good energy. They taste chocolatey, but no chocolate in them – weird.'

BEN COLEBY – 'Lucy made me a batch to take on bike rides. I soon worked my way through them – perfect energy boost. I saw the recipe (no baking) so had a go – easy. Mine would not win prizes to look at but they tasted good.'

DI PALUMBO – 'I take my cycling seriously and am very conscious of what I eat to keep my energy levels up. These are made with pure ingredients, give me a real boost without relying on packaged energy drinks and gels, and I also just love the taste.'

TIP

YOU CAN MAKE THESE BARS AS SMOOTH OR AS ROUGH-TEXTURED AS YOU LIKE.

KNEADING, PROVING, RESTING, SPONGING AND SO THE YEAST DOUGH JARGON GOES ON — FEAR NOT — IF YOU ARE A NOVICE TO BREAD MAKING I HOPE THIS CHAPTER WILL ENCOURAGE YOU TO HAVE A GO AND TO DISPEL SOME OLD BAKING MYTHS. IF YOU ARE AN EXPERT, I HOPE THIS CHAPTER WILL HAVE SOME FRESH IDEAS THAT WILL INSPIRE YOU TO BAKE SOMETHING DIFFERENT. MY AIM FOR BREAD MAKING — LESS CHORE, MORE AMOUR — HOPE YOU LIKE IT! MAKE SURE YOU READ MY TIPS ON MAKING GREAT BREAD OVERLEAF BEFORE YOU GET STARTED.

BREAD

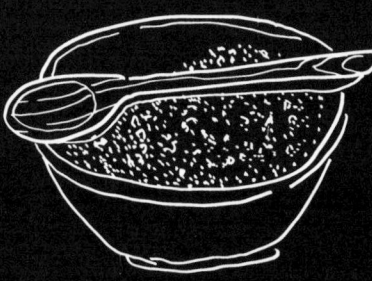

FOR THE LOVE OF BREAD

Read this before you try my bread recipes…

The thing about yeast-based bread is that you need to enjoy making it. I learnt to bake bread when I did my chef training but without a love for it I was never a successful baker. I now believe it was simply for that reason – it is not about loving bread in itself, as I am not a big bread eater but it is about loving the process. It's the sheer joy of the perfect rise, the satisfaction of baking bread your way and there is little in this world to beat the heady, yeasty smell as it cooks. Follow the tips here before you start baking.

Bread-making can seem a mystery: proving, sponging, kneading, resting – so much technique, where is the room for love? So much later when I learned to bake bread again – this time in France – there seemed less mystery and a bit more 'amour' to it all.

I don't want to bake bread every day, nor do I want to have to plan my baking, I just want to make bread when I fancy it. So my aim was to create some recipes that did just that. I use ingredients I can store and have simplified my bread to several core recipes that can be varied to make a number of different bakes.

The kneading is quite different in France and although you may find traditional British kneading a better process for you, I have found the French way excellent in preventing me from adding too much extra flour to the dough and so I get a lighter, better risen loaf.

Something to learn early on is that the temperature in which you leave bread to rise is critical – it simply takes much longer if it is cold – so I also suggest places to let dough rise and tips to find out how best to make bread in your home no matter where you live. Above all it is my aim to remove some of the fuss and allow bread-making to seem more accessible to those unfamiliar with all that 'baking with yeast' business.

I am sure there are some traditional and expert bakers whose hair will stand on end at some of what I say and do. But, hey ho, this is the way I make my bread and it's the way I've learned to love it. I hope very much that if you have never been tempted to try, then this will encourage you to give it a go and grow to love it too.

Included in this section are also some of the other Lucy's soda breads which are just fantastic – no yeast, quick bakes that are deeply and instantly satisfying. They have no rules, they are just mix and bake! These are great recipes to start with as you'll see almost instant results. To kick off your yeast bread-making, I'd recommend the Polenta Bread to make a Focaccia on page 148, and Potato and Onion Seed Loaf on page 143.

MY GOLDEN RULES FOR MAKING GREAT BREAD

1. Always weigh out your ingredients carefully and accurately. I am convinced this is important. I use digital scales and also I weigh my liquid. I don't measure it in a jug as I think it is hard to be accurate in volume, so all my recipes have liquid as a weight not a volume measurement. If you don't have digital scales just use the same quantity but in millilitres. So if I call for 250 g (9 oz) water, you can measure 250 ml (9 fl oz).

2. Never use ordinary cake-baking flour – you really do need strong bread flour. It contains more gluten and releases this more easily so your bread takes less kneading to get the elastic textured dough you need for it to rise well.

3. Never add extra flour when you're kneading. Adding more flour than the recipe calls for makes bread heavy and solid. If you are getting in a really sticky mess, just use a bit of oil on your hands and work surface (not much, just a drop).

4. What yeast to use? I have listed fast-action

(instant) dried yeast in all my recipes. This is because where I live it is not easy to buy fresh yeast and these are storecupboard recipes. If you have fresh yeast, simply rub it into the flour using your fingers and thumbs until it is like breadcrumbs before adding the rest of the ingredients. I use the same weight of fresh yeast to fast-action dried yeast and it seems to be fine.

5 Temperature – yeast is alive. Baking bread at a hot temperature kills the yeast and stops the bread rising, so you want the loaf risen to its full height before you bake it. You can stop the yeast working by freezing it, but this does not kill it. So fresh yeast and sourdough starters can be frozen, defrosted and brought back to room temperature then they will continue to do their job where they left off. At temperatures in between freezing and killing, yeast will create bubbles and the speed of this process is determined by the temperature. You need to allow this to happen – called proving – to make your bread rise. If you want your bread as soon as you possibly can, then place the bread to prove (rise) in a warm room, the airing cupboard, somewhere near an Aga-style oven, on a shelf over a radiator or even on a floor if under-heated – all perfect. My house is a little cool for making bread so I heat the oven to its lowest setting (60°C/140°F). Gas ovens don't go that low but you can set it to ¼ and leave the door slightly open. Put the dough in there and it will happily double in size in about 30 minutes. If you have a busy life and need to divide your bread-making into smaller time slots, you can easily let your dough rise in a cool place or the fridge overnight. By altering the temperature of the 'rise' you can fit bread-making into almost any lifestyle.

6 Kneading – see my tips on kneading overleaf, but the aim is to develop the gluten in the bread to give a supple, elastic, non-sticky dough.

7 Some breads don't need a second rise. You can simply knead, shape, prove, then bake some bread dough, but usually you allow the dough to double in size, 'knock' it back to the original size then shape and allow the dough to rise again before baking. This helps the texture of the bread.

8 Your oven – I prefer a fan oven for best, even results but I have put normal temperatures in the recipes to suit everyone. If you have a fan oven, use it and reduce the temperature accordingly (see the chart on page 9).

9 Bread is cooked when it sounds hollow when you tap it with your knuckle on the base of the loaf. If you do not get a hollow sound, pop it back into the oven for a few more minutes.

10 The crust of the bread is always better if you put a ramekin or similar small ovenproof dish of water in the oven with it while it's baking.

11 Hot bread straight from the oven – what could be better? But advice suggests you should always allow the bread to cool, on a rack, before eating – the crusts are crustier and I actually think that the texture of bread is better if the loaf is left uncut till it's cool. You can always warm your bread to serve!

BREAD MAKING STEP-BY-STEP

1. MIX THE INGREDIENTS TOGETHER LOOSELY WITH A FORK IN THE MIXING BOWL SO THEY BEGIN TO HOLD TOGETHER IN A ROUGH DOUGH.

2. TURN THE ROUGH MIXTURE ONTO A CLEAN WORK SURFACE AND USE YOUR HANDS TO DRAW IT TOGETHER INTO A DOUGH. IT WILL BE STICKY.

3. HOLD THE DOUGH IN ONE OR TWO HANDS AND THROW IT TOWARDS THE WORK SURFACE KEEPING HOLD OF THE END NEAREST YOU SO THAT IT SLAPS DOWN AND EXTENDS AWAY FROM YOU. IT WILL BE A STICKY THWACK.

4. SCOOP THE DOUGH UP, FOLD IT OVER ON TOP OF ITSELF TO FORM A ROUGH BALL THEN KEEP REPEATING THE THROW AND FOLD FOR ABOUT 7 MINUTES UNTIL SMOOTH AND ELASTIC.

5. START TO SHAPE THE DOUGH INTO A BALL. HOLD THE EDGE AWAY FROM YOU AND LIFT IT AND BRING IT TO THE CENTRE PRESSING IT DOWN TO STICK ONTO THE REST OF THE DOUGH. TURN THE BALL ABOUT 15 DEGREES AND DO THE SAME, THEN WORK YOUR WAY ROUND THE PIECE AND YOU WILL HAVE A NEAT BALL.

6. FLIP THE BALL OVER AND PUT IT BACK IN THE MIXING BOWL TO RISE OR SHAPE IT FOR YOUR SOURDOUGH MOULD OR LOAF. COVER WITH A TEA (DISH) TOWEL AND LEAVE TO PROVE (SEE TIPS ON PAGE 133). IF THE RECIPE STATES, RE-KNEAD THEN SHAPE AND LEAVE UNTIL DOUBLED IN SIZE AGAIN.

TIP

GOOD BREAD DOUGH IS WETTER THAN YOU THINK. THIS IS THE BEST WAY TO KNEAD DOUGH, TO KEEP THAT ESSENTIAL MOISTURE LOCKED IN.

BRIOCHE MADE SIMPLE

PREPARATION 10 mins + proving

COOKING 25 mins

MAKES 1 round or oblong loaf

VEGETARIAN

NUT-FREE

This recipe is inspired by a French friend – she adds orange blossom water (also known as orange flower water) to the liquid and it adds a floral, sweet flavour that is only just detectable but is quite exceptional. So I now add it to mine and I hope that you now will add it to yours but it works well without it, so don't wait to buy some before you have a go at this! I also cheat madly in this recipe and rub the butter into the flour like cake making before I start to make the bread – it is so easy and the result is fabulous – a wonderful weekend breakfast treat.

150 g (5 oz) butter, at room temperature
500 g (1 lb 2 oz/4 cups) strong white bread flour
12 g (½ oz) fast-action (instant) dried yeast
3 g (⅛ oz) salt
50 g (2 oz/¼ cup) caster (superfine) sugar
150 g (5 oz) milk
2 eggs
5 g (¼ oz) orange blossom (orange flower) water

FOR THE GLAZE
50 g (2 oz/scant ½ cup) icing (confectioners') sugar
10 g (½ oz) water

1. Line a 20 cm (8 in) deep round cake tin or 1 kg (2 lb) loaf tin with baking paper.
2. Chop the butter into small pieces and put it into your mixing bowl with the flour, yeast, salt and sugar.
3. Using your fingers and thumbs, rub the butter into the dry ingredients until it resembles breadcrumbs.
4. Warm the milk for 30 seconds on full power in the microwave, just to take the chilled edge off it, and then add the eggs and orange blossom water to the milk and mix well. Add to the dry ingredients, mix together to a dough and turn out onto a clean work surface.
5. Knead as the bread notes describe on page 134 for 7 minutes. Divide the dough into 6 parts and shape each into a ball as directed in the step-by-step notes on page 134. Put 1 ball in the centre of the tin and place the others evenly around the edge. Cover with a clean tea towel and leave until doubled in size (I place it in my oven at 60°C/140°F, or Gas ¼ with the door slightly ajar, for 30 minutes, but see tips on how to speed up or slow down proving loaves on page 133).
6. Preheat the oven to 200°C (400°F/Gas 6) – taking the loaf out first if you are proving the loaf in it!
7. Bake the brioche for 25 minutes. Blend the icing sugar with the water until smooth. Turn the loaf out onto a wire rack and brush immediately with the sugar glaze. Leave to cool.

WHAT THE TESTERS SAY

JACQUI MELVILLE AND SUZANNE QUINTNER – 'This was much less messy than we thought it would be – I always thought brioche took a lot of technique but we had fun making this together.'

KERRY GREGORY – 'Wow! We had it toasted with paté – wonderful combo!'

HATTIE CUFFLIN – 'This was easy – I made 4 balls of dough and stuck them in a row in a 1 kg (2 lb) loaf tin to make a beautiful loaf. I took it to my sister's for the weekend, sliced it, toasted it and we ate it with jam on a Sunday morning.'

TIP

ALTHOUGH THIS IS A SLIGHTLY SWEET BREAD, IT MAKES GREAT TOAST TO SERVE WITH A ROUGH GOOD QUALITY PÂTÉ OR TERRINE.

SOURDOUGH STARTER

PREPARATION	COOKING	MAKES	VEGETARIAN	NUT-FREE
10 mins	40 mins	1 large loaf		

The initial 'starter' takes 5 days, but you freeze it, defrost and re-feed it, so the next time the process is quicker. It is a labour of love but worth it. I use yoghurt and milk to give it a quick start but you can just use water.

FOR THE SOURDOUGH STARTER

DAY 1
175 g (6 oz) milk
150 g (5 oz) live plain yoghurt
120 g (4 oz/1 cup) strong white bread flour

DAY 2
150 g (5 oz/1¼ cups) strong white bread flour
150 g (5 oz) water

DAY 4
150 g (5 oz/1¼ cups) strong white bread flour
150 g (5 oz) water

DAY 5
150 g (5 oz/1¼ cups) strong white bread flour
150 g (5 oz) water

DAY 1
Heat the milk in a saucepan until just boiling and then remove from the heat and stir in the yoghurt. Add the flour, put it in a bowl, cover with a tea (dish) towel and leave overnight at room temperature (allowing plenty of air space to draw yeast from).

DAY 2
Stir in the flour and water and repeat the process as day 1 but leave for 2 days.

DAY 4
Add the flour and water, mix well and leave again for 24 hours as day 1.

DAY 5
As day 4 – the mix will have turned a sort of grey colour and have bubbles in it.

DAY 6
The starter is ready to use. Measure out the 300 g (10½ oz) of starter for the loaf and then either freeze the rest if you are not making bread again for a while or you can store the remainder in the fridge. This will slow the process but you will still need to feed your starter every couple of days with equal quantities of flour and water to keep it alive. Now you are ready to make your own sourdough loaf.

SOURDOUGH BREAD

PREPARATION	COOKING	MAKES	VEGETARIAN	NUT-FREE
20 mins + overnight rise	40 mins	1 large loaf		

I call this my friendly bread because I often share my starter dough with friends and family. The loaf has a fabulous chewy, open texture, sour flavour and, I think, is the king of loaves. Sourdough has no added yeast but you make a paste with flour and liquid and leave it exposed to the air and as it sours it draws natural yeasts from the air and ferments.

500 g (1 lb 2 oz/4 cups) strong white bread flour
300 g (10½ oz) sourdough starter (see page 139)
250 g (9 oz) water
10 g (½ oz) sugar
10 g (½ oz) salt

1 Mix together the flour, sourdough starter, water, sugar and salt using a fork until you have a rough dough.
2 Turn it out onto a clean work surface and knead for 7 minutes as described on page 134 or until you have a non-sticky, elastic dough.
3 This dough is softer than other breads and really needs a mould to help it keep shape to rise. You can buy a 'banneton' (a bread basket-shaped container for proving bread), which you flour liberally or simply line a baking dish or tin with baking paper. I use a 20 cm (8 in) square, deep cake tin and this makes a great square deep loaf (*pavé* as the French would call it).
4 Turn your soft dough into your mould, sprinkle liberally with flour, score some lines on the top using a sharp knife and then cover it with a tea towel. I always leave my sourdough overnight to rise as it likes a slower, cooler temperature rise.
5 Heat the oven to 230°C (450°F/Gas 8) and put a ramekin or similar small dish of water in the oven. If using a banneton, quickly turn the loaf out onto a baking paper-lined baking tray. Bake the loaf for 10 minutes at this temperature then turn the oven down to 220°C (430°F/Gas 7) and bake for a further 30 minutes, or until the bread is a good brown colour.
6 Turn the loaf out of the tin, if using, and knock on the base of the loaf with your fist. If it sounds hollow then the bread is ready. Cool on a wire rack before slicing.

WHAT THE TESTERS SAY

DI PALUMBO – 'Inheriting a pot of the starter from Lucy I got cracking straight away. I kneaded and left my dough to prove on Saturday night, baking fresh bread for my houseguests on the Sunday morning. They were amazed I had got up and baked bread but all I did that morning was pop it into the oven. I have now made it 4 times, 7 minutes kneading each time and perfect bread that I am really proud of. I used wholemeal flour for mine.'

BRENDAN CROFT – 'I was given the starter which made it easy as a first go and it worked amazingly – so now I am starting from scratch but I am hooked.'

JANET MEEKCOMS – 'I made this most days when I was staying in France so I kept my sourdough starter well-fed and alive on the kitchen worktop. The flavour of the bread is wonderful and kneading quick. You need to put the bread into a mould, though, as it spreads out when rising.'

TIP
WHEN MAKING THE BREAD, YOU CAN USE 100 G RYE FLOUR IN PLACE OF THE 100 G OF THE STRONG WHITE FLOUR.

EASY SPELT BREAD

PREPARATION 10 mins + proving | **COOKING** 35–40 mins | **MAKES** 1 large loaf or 2 smaller loaves | **VEGETARIAN** | **DAIRY-FREE**

Spelt is the wild ancestor of our common wheat flour today. It's one of the easiest flours to use as it kneads quickly and rises fast and its flavour is fabulous. I recommend you try this early in your bread-making journey as I am pretty sure you'll be happy with the results – it is a one-rise loaf, so no excessive waiting around is necessary. You can use all spelt flour but the texture will be a little heavier. This makes a good rustic loaf when plain but is very happy for nuts, seeds or spices to be added to it so let your imagination loose.

400 g (14 oz/4 cups) spelt flour
100 g (3½ oz/generous ¾ cup) strong white bread flour
15 g (½ oz) fast-action (instant) dried yeast
10 g (½ oz) salt
100 g (3½ oz/generous ¾ cup) chopped walnuts (optional)
320 g (11½ oz) warm water
20 g (¾ oz) clear honey
50 g (2 oz) olive oil

1. Line a baking sheet with baking paper.
2. Stir the flours, dried yeast, salt and nuts, if using, together.
3. Add the water, honey and olive oil to the bowl and mix together using a fork to a rough dough.
4. Turn out onto a clean work surface and follow the instructions for kneading on page 134. The dough needs to be wet to start with and elastic when you are ready to shape it. This should take about 7–10 minutes. Once kneaded, sprinkle a little flour on the work surface and bring your dough to a round shape by folding the outsides in and turning the dough ball at each fold over (see page 134). You will have a nice round ball.
5. Turn the ball over onto the baking sheet and sprinkle with white flour. Put a clean tea towel over the top and leave it until doubled in size (I place it in my oven at 60°C/140°F, or Gas ¼ with the door slightly ajar, for 30 minutes, but see tips on how to speed up or slow down proving loaves on page 133). . Wait for it to double or the bread will be heavy.
6. Preheat the oven to 220°C (430°F/Gas 7) – take the loaf out first if proving in it!
7. Bake for 35–40 minutes – you can tell the loaf is done by knocking with your fist on the bottom of the bread and then it should sound hollow. Transfer to a wire rack to cool.

WHAT THE TESTERS SAY

MARK SCILLEY – 'It took me three attempts to get a texture that I was proud of. I had not kneaded it enough but now I have the hang of it I bake it all the time. The loaf lasts well for several days and makes excellent toast.'

IAN MEEKCOMS – 'I have made white bread before but found spelt really easy to work with – one rise, so simple!'

TIP

TRY USING HALF WATER AND HALF BEER FOR A DIFFERENT FLAVOUR.

POTATO AND ONION SEED BREAD

PREPARATION
10 mins + proving

COOKING
35 mins

MAKES
1 loaf

VEGAN & VEGETARIAN

NUT-FREE

DAIRY-FREE

Subtly seedy, squishy, soft and easy-peasy – this is a bread you can make as a novice and will never stop making – and, yes, it has mashed potato in it! I always line my loaf tins with baking paper as I love the way they just plop out at the end with no worry but, of course, you can just grease your tin if you prefer.

300 g (10½ oz) potatoes (peeled weight)
10 g (½ oz) fast-action (instant) dried yeast
10 g (½ oz) caster (superfine) sugar
15 g (½ oz) olive oil
7 g (¼ oz) salt
250 g (9 oz/2 cups) strong white bread flour
100 g (3½ oz/⅔ cup) wholemeal (whole wheat) bread flour
20 g (¾ oz) black onion seeds (nigella seeds)

1. Line a 1 kg (2 lb) loaf tin with baking paper.
2. Peel, chop and cook the potatoes in unsalted water for 15 minutes or until cooked. Drain, reserving the water. Mash the potatoes over a low heat to remove excess water.
3. Put the rest of the ingredients into a bowl, add the potatoes and then 75 g (2½ oz) of the potato cooking water.
4. Mix with a fork until you have a rough dough and turn the mixture out onto a clean work surface. Bring it together and knead for 7 minutes (see page 134). The dough should now be much less sticky, more elastic and ready to rise.
5. Sprinkle a little flour on the surface now and shape the dough into a ball (see page 134). Put it back into the mixing bowl and cover it with a tea towel. Leave it to prove and double in size (I place it in my oven at 60°C/140°F, or Gas ¼ with the door slightly ajar, for 30 minutes, but see tips on how to speed up or slow down proving loaves on page 133). Turn it back onto the work surface, knead it back to the original size then dust the work surface with a little flour and shape it into a fat sausage to fit into the loaf tin. Cover with a tea towel.
6. Leave in a warm place (the oven or room temperature) to rise again. Preheat the oven to 220°C (430°F/Gas 7) – take the loaf out first if proving in there!
7. Bake for 35 minutes until risen, crisp and browned. You can tell the loaf is done by turning it out and knocking the base with your fist – it should sound hollow.

WHAT THE TESTERS SAY

NAOMI HULME – 'This is a light and excellent bread. I used poppy and let it rise in the oven at 60°C (140°F/Gas ¼) , which was a revelation to me – fantastic!'

SAMUEL RAFTER – 'It was so quick to make because the cooking liquid and potatoes are hot when the dough is being kneaded. I will make it again.'

From left to right: Polenta Bread Focaccia, Easy Spelt Bread, Polenta Bread Sticks, Potato and Onion Seed Bread, Paddy's Beer Bread, Seeded Wholemeal Bread

SEEDED WHOLEMEAL BREAD

PREPARATION
30 mins + proving

COOKING
30 mins

MAKES
1 loaf

VEGETARIAN

DAIRY-FREE

This is a hefty loaf full of goodness. Don't start with this if you are a novice because wholemeal flours are a bit trickier to work with. This is a good, basic wholemeal loaf, though, and you can swap and change the flavours within the recipe (see below). The fennel seeds make this bread. You can hunt them out at Asian grocers or online if your supermarket doesn't have them and you can even roast your own by simply tossing raw fennel seeds in turmeric and dry-roasting on a baking tray at 200°C (400°F/Gas 6) for about 5 minutes. Try pumpkin or sunflower seeds in place of walnuts, too. See the picture of the loaf on page 145.

400 g (14 oz/2⅔ cups) strong wholemeal bread flour
100 g (3½ oz/generous ¾ cup) strong white bread flour
15 g (½ oz) fast-action (instant) dried yeast
10 g (½ oz) salt
100 g (3½ oz/generous ¾ cup) walnut pieces, roughly chopped
3 g (⅛ oz) roasted fennel seeds
30 g (1 oz) clear honey
400 g (14 oz) warm water

1. Line a baking sheet with paper. Put the flours, yeast, salt, nuts and seeds into a large bowl and stir well.
2. Stir the honey and water into the flour mixture with a fork to start to mix to a rough dough.
3. Turn onto a lightly floured surface and bring together to a dough then knead (see bread making notes on page 134) until elastic and no longer sticky. Return it to the bowl, cover with a tea towel and leave to prove until doubled in size (I place it in my oven at 60°C/140°F, or Gas ¼ with the door slightly ajar, for 30 minutes, but see tips on how to speed up or slow down proving loaves on page 133).
4. Return the risen dough to the work surface and knead again to reduce it to the original size and shape into a round loaf (see page 134). Place on the prepared baking sheet, dust with flour and then score a cross in the top with a very sharp knife.
5. Cover again with the tea towel and leave to rise again in a warm place (back in the oven or at room temperature) until doubled in size.
6. Preheat the oven to 230°C (450°F/Gas 8) – take the loaf out first if proving in there. Bake for 30 minutes, reducing the temperature after 10 minutes to 220°C (430°F/Gas 7).
7. Knock the base of the loaf with your fist and if it sounds hollow the loaf is done. Cool completely on a wire rack before cutting.

WHAT THE TESTER SAYS

BEN COLEBY – 'I love grainy loaves. This was my first ever bread-making, so it took me some time and advice to understand the textures. I then made the polenta bread and should have started with that one and moved on to this one. But I now have the hang of it and make it in the evening – a great de-stress from work. I bake it in a loaf tin and it makes delicious toast and sandwiches.'

PADDY'S BEER BREAD

PREPARATION	COOKING	VEGETARIAN	NUT-FREE	DAIRY-FREE
10 mins + proving	30 mins			

Paddy, a friend whose real name is Mark, incidentally, has fond memories of Veda loaf while he was growing up in Northern Ireland. But as we were in France when we tried to recreate this childhood memory we had no access to its main ingredient – malt extract. We improvised and used beer in place of water to give us that malty taste and after a couple of attempts were very happy with this beery, dark bread. It makes wonderful toast and is great sliced to serve with soup. Not really like Veda loaf at all but we actually think this is a terrific bread with a dark cinnamon colour. See the picture of the loaf on page 143.

500 g (1 lb 2 oz) strong white bread flour
10 g (½ oz) fast-action (instant) dried yeast
10 g (½ oz) salt
30 g (1 oz) olive oil or rapeseed oil
50 g (2 oz) black treacle (molasses)
300 ml (10½ oz) malty brown beer

1. Line a 1 kg (2 lb) loaf tin with baking paper.
2. Put the flour, yeast and salt into a large bowl and mix well.
3. Add the oil, treacle and the beer and stir with a fork to start to mix.
4. Turn it onto a clean work surface and follow the kneading notes on page 134. Return it to the bowl, cover with a tea (dish) towel and leave it until doubled in size (I place it in my oven at 60°C/140°F, or Gas ¼ with the door slightly ajar, for 30 minutes, but see tips on speeding up or slowing down proving on page 133).
5. When the dough has doubled in size, return it to the work surface and knead again to reduce it to the original size and then shape into an oblong and put it in the prepared tin.
6. Cover again with a tea towel and leave to rise again in the oven or at room temperature until it has doubled in size.
7. Preheat the oven to 220°C (430°F/Gas 7) – take the bread out first if proving in it! Bake for 30 minutes adding a ramekin of water to the oven.
8. Knock on the bottom with your fist – if it sounds hollow the loaf is done. Cool completely before cutting into slices.

WHAT THE TESTERS SAY

MARK SCILLEY – 'It's not like the Veda bread of my youth in Northern Ireland but I love this beery dark loaf.'

IAN MEEKCOMS AND FAMILY – 'I have never tried Veda loaf, so I don't know what it was meant to be like, but we love this bread – I have it with salty butter and oysters.'

LIZ EVERSON – 'I had no idea what this would be like. It is dark and slightly sweet. A good toasting bread.'

TIP
SPEND AN EXTRA COUPLE OF MINUTES KNEADING TO ENSURE YOU HAVE A REALLY ELASTIC DOUGH.

POLENTA BREAD

| PREPARATION | COOKING | VEGAN & | NUT- | DAIRY- |
| 10 mins + proving and shaping | 10–30 mins | VEGETARIAN | FREE | FREE |

Finding ourselves in an authentic Italian restaurant my son and I ordered some focaccia and oil to start with while we talked about the university we had just visited. The bread took ages but when it came it was fresh from the brick oven and unbelievably light. On asking I was told the secret to very light bread is to add some finely ground polenta to the dough, so I removed some flour and added some polenta and here is the result. This bread is great for bread novices as the results is a super light super gratifying bread that works every time.

475 g (1 lb 2 oz/scant 4 cups) strong white bread flour
50 g (2 oz/⅓ cup) fine polenta or cornmeal
15 g (½ oz) fast-action (instant) dried yeast
10 g (½ oz) salt
320 g (11½ oz) warm water
50 g (2 oz) olive oil

1. Put the flour, polenta, dried yeast and salt into a bowl and mix together so the yeast is evenly distributed.
2. Add the water and olive oil and stir the mix together with a fork until it starts to come together, then turn it out onto a clean work surface and bring it together to a wet dough.
3. Follow the kneading notes on page 134 at this point. I put the radio on and listen to two tracks and it is done! Put the floured, kneaded dough ball back into your bowl, cover with a tea (dish) towel and leave to prove in a warm place until doubled in size (I place it in my oven at 60°C/140°F, or Gas ¼ with the door slightly ajar, for 30 minutes, but see tips on how to speed up or slow down proving loaves on page 133).
4. Shape into focaccia (see opposite), pizzas, a loaf in a 1 kg (2 lb) loaf tin, or 12 rolls on a lined baking sheet. Alternatively for breadsticks, divide the dough in half. For slim ones roll the dough to 1 cm (½ in) thick and cut into 5 mm (¼ in) wide strips. For fat sticks roll out a little thicker and cut into 1.5 cm (⅝ in) wide strips. Place them a little apart on baking sheets lined with baking paper.
5. Except for the pizza, leave the shaped bread to rise until doubled in size again (in the oven or at room temperature).
6. Preheat the oven to 220°C (430°F/Gas 7) – take the bread out first if proving in there! Bake for 10–15 minutes for breadsticks, 15 minutes for rolls or 30 minutes for loaves. Cool on a wire rack.
7. For the pizza, bake for 5 minutes to crisp the base. Slide it onto the hot sheet on the top shelf. Use a cold baking sheet to transfer another pizza on to the oven floor. Bake 5 minutes more. Remove the top pizza and keep warm. Move the second pizza up to the hot baking sheet place another on the oven floor. Continue until all are cooked.

ALTERNATIVE COOKING TIMES AND YIELDS

PIZZAS – 5–10 minutes/makes 4 large pizzas
BREADSTICKS AND ROLLS – 10–15 minutes/makes about 50 breadsticks or 12 rolls (see picture on page 144)
FOCACCIA – 20 minutes/makes 2 flat focaccias
LOAVES – 30 minutes/makes 1 large loaf

WHAT THE TESTERS SAY

HATTIE CUFFLIN – 'I've never made bread. This worked for me – I could not believe it. I used 125 g (4 oz/1 cup) rye flour and 400 g (14 oz/generous 3 cups) white bread flour and made giant rolls for my homemade burgers.'

FOCACCIA STEP-BY-STEP

1. FOLLOWING ON FROM STEP 3 (OPPOSITE), RE-KNEAD THE PROVED DOUGH AND DIVIDE IT INTO 2 BALLS. ON A LIGHTLY FLOURED SURFACE, ROLL EACH PIECE OUT USING A FLOURED ROLLING PIN INTO A RECTANGLE. PLACE IN 2 OILED 18 X 28 CM (7 X 11 IN) BAKING TIN.

2. USING YOUR FINGERTIPS, PRESS THE DOUGH GENTLY BUT FIRMLY RIGHT OUT TO THE CORNERS OF EACH TIN (IT WILL BE VERY ELASTIC SO PERSEVERE). IT SHOULD EVENLY HALF-FILL THE TIN.

3. USING A PAIR OF SCISSORS, SNIP ALL OVER THE SURFACE OF THE DOUGH TO MAKE LITTLE DENTS IN IT. POKE SOME CHOPPED FRESH ROSEMARY INTO THE SLITS, IF LIKED.

4. BRUSH WITH A LITTLE WATER AND SCATTER COARSE SEA SALT (OR CHILLI OR OTHER FLAVOURED SALT, IF PREFERRED) OVER THE SURFACE. COVER WITH THE TEA TOWEL AND LEAVE TO RISE AGAIN UNTIL DOUBLED IN SIZE. PREHEAT THE OVEN TO 220°C (430°F/GAS 7).

BAKE FOR 20 MINUTES UNTIL THE BASE SOUNDS HOLLOW WHEN KNOCKED. LEAVE IN THE TIN, DRIZZLE WITH 100 G (3½ OZ) OLIVE OIL AND ADD SOME CRUSHED GARLIC IF LIKED. LEAVE TO SOAK AND SERVE WARM.

PIZZA STEP-BY-STEP

1. DIVIDE THE RE-KNEADED, PROVED DOUGH INTO QUARTERS AND SHAPE INTO BALLS. ROLL EACH OUT ON A SHEET OF BAKING PAPER TO A THIN DISC, TURNING THE PAPER REGULARLY TO KEEP THE ROUND SHAPE.

2. PUSH THE EDGES ALL ROUND WITH THE FINGERTIPS TO NEATEN AND SLIGHTLY RAISE THE EDGE. MAKE A QUICK TOMATO SAUCE: BLEND A 400 G (14 OZ) CAN CHOPPED TOMATOES WITH A FINELY GRATED GARLIC CLOVE, 50 G (2 OZ) OLIVE OIL, 1 TABLESPOON TOMATO PURÉE, 1 TEASPOON SUGAR, SALT AND PEPPER.

3. SLIDE 1 PIZZA ON ITS PAPER ONTO A BAKING SHEET. SPREAD THE TOMATO SAUCE THINLY OVER ALL THE PIZZA BASES, NOT QUITE TO THE EDGES, USING THE BACK OF A WOODEN SPOON.

4. IF USING MORE TOPPINGS (MUSHROOMS, PEPPERS, HAM, OLIVES ETC.), ADD THEM NOW BEFORE THE CHEESE. FOR A SIMPLE MARGHERITA PIZZA, SIMPLY SPRINKLE EVENLY WITH GRATED MOZZARELLA.

5. TAKE A SMALL BUNCH OF FRESH BASIL LEAVES AND SCATTER OVER THE SURFACE. SEASON WITH PLENTY OF FRESHLY GROUND BLACK PEPPER AND A SPRINKLING OF SEA SALT. PREHEAT THE OVEN AS HOT AS IT GOES. HEAT A BAKING SHEET ON THE TOP SHELF.

6. DRIZZLE A LITTLE OLIVE OIL OVER THE PIZZAS. SLIDE THE ONE ON THE BAKING SHEET OFF ON TO THE ACTUAL BASE OF THE OVEN JUST ON ITS PAPER. SEE PAGE 148 FOR BAKING INSTRUCTIONS.

TIGER TEA LOAF

| PREPARATION | COOKING | MAKES | VEGAN & | DAIRY- |
| 10 mins + soaking | 1 hour | 1 small loaf | VEGETARIAN | FREE |

This is a variant of my mother's miracle tea bread – the ingredients and method are so simple it's hard to believe you can make something so delicious with so little effort. I use a mix of beer and Earl Grey tea but you can use all beer or all tea if you prefer. I first used beer local to me in Leicester – Everards Tiger Ale – and so that's how it got its name. It is made for slicing and buttering and enjoying with a cuppa but, equally, it can go butterless in a pocket to sustain on a long walk! Using a standard tea mug will make a 500 g (1 lb 2 oz) loaf. Dates tend to 'disappear' in the loaf when cooked but give a great taste and texture and, nutritionally, are still there even if you can't see them!

1 mugful of All-Bran cereal
1 mugful of demerara (raw) sugar
1 mugful of mixed dried fruit and nuts
½ mugful of Earl Grey tea made with 2 bags left to brew but still warm
½ mugful real ale
1 mugful of self-raising flour

TIP
YOU CAN USE ANY MIX OF FRUIT AND NUTS FOR THIS LOAF.

1 In a large bowl mix the All-Bran, sugar, dried fruit and nuts and add the warm tea (minus the teabags) and the ale.
2 Stir well, cover and leave for 2 hours or overnight.
3 Preheat the oven to 160°C (320°F/Gas 3) and line a 500 g (1 lb 2 oz) loaf tin with baking paper.
4 Mix the flour into the soaked mixture.
5 Turn into the prepared tin and bake for 1 hour or until firm on the top.
6 Remove from the tin, remove the baking paper and wrap in cling film (plastic wrap) while still warm to help it stay really moist.
7 It's best kept for a few days to allow the flavours to develop and can be stored in an airtight container for up to 1 month.

WHAT THE TESTERS SAY

ALANDA WHITEHEAD – 'I served it for Easter Sunday tea with friends and made it with two-thirds Earl Grey tea and a third ale, and threw in some dried cherries and apricots. It was a lovely moist cake.'

NAOMI HULME – 'This has become one of my favourite tea time treats – excellent for non-dairy eaters. I have also made it with porridge oats in place of All-Bran and called it oaf!'

JANET MEEKCOMS – 'How this makes a tea bread I do not know. One week on, the loaf is sticky, sweet and perfect with a cup of tea. I used a sugar substitute and it worked really well.'

TIP
YOU CAN MAKE THIS LOAF VEGAN AND DAIRY-FREE BY CHANGING THE FILLING.

PICNIC LOAF

PREPARATION	COOKING	MAKES	VEGETARIAN	NUT-FREE
10 mins + proving	30 mins	1 loaf		

This loaf is made with my polenta bread recipe, which is a basic bread dough, but filled with gorgeous flavours. It is perfect to make and take with you for a great picnic or warm it through for a casual lunch. I've used the classic flavours of sun-dried tomatoes, spinach, cheese and the delicious fragrance of basil. However, it can be adapted easily to make it your own by choosing your favourite cheese, adding meats, greens and different herbs.

½ x 280 g (10 oz) jar of sun-dried tomatoes in oil, drained (or 75 g (2½ oz) drained homemade ones, see page 195), plus a little of the oil
4 handfuls of fresh spinach leaves, chopped
1 garlic clove, grated finely
200 g (7 oz/1⅔ cups) grated cheese of your choice
salt and freshly ground black pepper
handful of basil leaves, torn
1 batch polenta bread dough, risen and ready to shape (see page 148)

1 Chop the drained tomatoes and mix well with the spinach and garlic. Add the cheese and moisten with a little oil from the tomatoes. Season to taste and stir in the basil.
2 Place the dough on a sheet of baking paper. Dust it with a little flour and roll the dough out to a rectangle about 30 x 25 cm (12 x 10 in). Slide the paper and dough onto a cold baking sheet (to help with handling later).
3 Pile the prepared filling down the centre third of the dough and spread it out, leaving about a 2 cm (8 in) strip of dough top and bottom.
4 Brush the uncovered dough with water to act as glue and fold one third over the filling and then the second third up and over the already folded side so you have a single layer of dough under the filling and a double layer on top.
5 Press the edges together to stop the filling oozing when baking. Cover with a tea towel and leave until doubled in size (I place it in my oven at 60°C/140°F, or Gas ¼ with the door slightly ajar, for 30 minutes, but see tips on how to speed up or slow down proving loaves on page 133).
6 Preheat the oven to 220°C (430°F/Gas 7) – take the loaf out first if proving in it – and put a baking sheet into the oven to get really hot.
7 Take the hot baking sheet from the oven. Quickly slide the bread onto it, return to the oven and bake for 30 minutes until risen, golden and cooked through. Eat warm, cut in slices, or leave until cold and pack up for a picnic.

WHAT THE TESTERS SAY

JO, JOSH AND BEN CURD – 'We love this polenta bread recipe and kneading it the French way is really fun – you can do it to music and dance along to the radio while you bake!'

IAN MEEKCOMS – 'This bread is easy and works every time. I fill mine with blue cheese and walnuts.'

RON SAWERS – 'This polenta bread recipe was not hard to follow. I filled it with a tomato sauce mixture, cheese and some herbs – my twin boys ate it all warm from the oven. A great idea for homemade bread.'

| VEGAN & VEGETARIAN | NUT-FREE | DAIRY-FREE |

LAGER LOAF

PREPARATION 5 mins | **COOKING** 1 hour | **MAKES** 1 loaf

One of Skiworld's American chalet hosts picked up a recipe from the Coors Brewery in Colorado after visiting it. Their beers are crisp, light and golden. The bread was nice enough but a few tweaks and adaptations later we have created a delicious soda bread that is so easy to make. It's a great loaf to slice or toast for breakfast but is equally good served with soup, cheese or pâté. It needs to be a mild lager or blond beer as bitter or brown beer would taste too strong.

200 g (7 oz/1⅓ cups) wholemeal (whole wheat) flour
200 g (7 oz/1⅔ cups) plain (all-purpose) white flour
400 g (14 oz) light-flavoured lager
30 g (1 oz/scant ¼ cup) caster (superfine) sugar
5 g (¼ oz) salt
7 g (¼ oz) baking powder
30 g (1 oz) olive oil

1. Line a 500 g (1 lb) loaf tin with baking paper and preheat the oven to 190°C (375°F/Gas 5).
2. Put all the ingredients into a bowl and mix to a soft, thick batter and pour into the prepared loaf tin.
3. Bake for 1 hour or until golden and risen and the base sounds hollow when the loaf is tipped out of the tin and tapped.
4. Wrap immediately in cling film (plastic wrap) as this helps soften the texture when cold. Store in an airtight container in the fridge for up to 5 days.

| VEGETARIAN | NUT-FREE |

PARMESAN CAKE

PREPARATION 15 mins | **COOKING** 30–35 mins | **MAKES** 1 loaf

This savoury cake (a Lucy LT's speciality) is simple to make, despite having to whisk the egg whites separately.

3 eggs, separated
150 g (5 oz) olive oil
170 g (6 oz) milk
50 g (2 oz/½ cup) freshly grated parmesan
3 g (⅛ oz) salt
freshly ground black pepper
200 g (7 oz/1⅔ cups) self-raising flour
3 g (⅛ oz) baking powder
50 g (2 oz/⅓ cup) fine semolina/cornmeal

1. Preheat the oven to 200°C (400°F/Gas 6). Line a 1 kg (2 lb) loaf tin with baking paper.
2. Whisk the egg whites until soft peaks, not stiff.
3. In another bowl, mix the eggs yolks, olive oil and milk. Stir in the Parmesan, salt and pepper. Sift the flour and baking powder, add the semolina and stir.
4. Mix a dollop of the whisked whites into the batter, to slacken the mixture, then fold in the remaining whites.
5. Turn into the prepared tin and bake for 30–35 minutes until golden brown and a cocktail stick or skewer inserted into the loaf comes out clean.
6. Cool in the tin, turn out and remove the paper. Store in an airtight container in the fridge for up to 5 days.

| VEGETARIAN | NUT-FREE |

CORNBREAD

PREPARATION 5 mins | **COOKING** 45–50 mins | **MAKES** 1 loaf

I have eaten Lucy LT's cornbread at her bar restaurant where she served it with a mean chilli – yum! Baking powder breads are a little more like cakes in texture and they lend themselves to many uses, which makes them perfect when time is short.

250 g (9 oz/2 cups) plain (all-purpose) flour
150 g (5 oz/1 cup) cornmeal
5 g (¼ oz) salt
10 g (½ oz) baking powder
50 g (2 oz/¼ cup) caster (superfine) sugar
150 g (5 oz) milk
200 g (7 oz) whole milk yoghurt
75 g (2½ oz) sunflower oil
2 eggs, beaten

1. Preheat oven to 220°C (430°F/Gas 7). Grease and line a 1 kg (2 lb) loaf tin with baking paper.
2. Put the dry ingredients into a mixing bowl and make a well in the centre.
3. Add the milk, yoghurt and oil and then the eggs to the well. Whisk until thick and smooth. Immediately spoon the batter into the prepared tin.
4. Bake for 45–50 minutes until golden and springy to the touch.
5. Cool on a wire rack or serve warm. Store in an airtight tin for up to 5 days or freeze for 6 months.

| VEGETARIAN | NUT-FREE |

SPEEDY SODA BREAD

PREPARATION 5 mins | **COOKING** 25 mins | **MAKES** 1 loaf

Anyone who's been to Ireland will know how lovely soda bread is for breakfast when fresh from the oven. Don't miss out the salt – this Lucy LT soda bread needs it.

200 g (7 oz/1⅓ cups) wholemeal (whole wheat) flour
250 g (9 oz/2 cups) plain (all-purpose) white flour, plus extra for dusting
6 g (¼ oz) bicarbonate of soda (baking soda)
6 g (¼ oz) salt
6 g (¼ oz) caster (superfine) sugar
5 g (¼ oz) lemon juice
350 g (12 oz) milk, plus extra if needed

1. Preheat the oven to 220°C (430°F/Gas 7). Oil a 20 cm (8 in) cake tin and dust with flour. Mix the 2 flours, bicarbonate of soda, salt and sugar in a bowl.
2. Add the lemon juice to the milk and quickly mix into the dry ingredients. The dough should be wet.
3. Working quickly, using floured hands, shape into a rough disc on a floured work surface and put into the tin, pressing into the corners.
4. Bake for 25 minutes until risen and brown and the base sounds hollow when knocked. Cool slightly on a wire rack. Best eaten warm and keeps for a day.

Baking does not need to be sweet to be a treat – what could be better than a few homemade biscuits sitting next to a piece of wonderfully ripe cheese or a little tasty morsel with a glass of wine? From oatcakes to retro olive bakes, indulge your savoury side with these scrumptious salty recipes. You can choose which flour you use and make these savouries as rustic or refined as your tastebuds demand. Before you get out the bowl, see page 8 for some extra tips to set you off on the right foot – happy baking!

SAVOURY

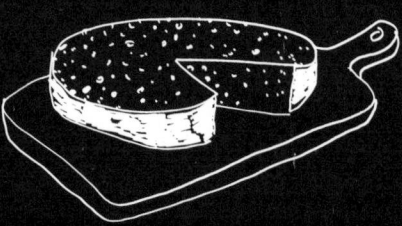

CHILLI CHEESE THINS

PREPARATION	COOKING	MAKES	VEGETARIAN	NUT-FREE
10 mins + chilling	10–12 mins	about 30 crisps		

We are Leicester girls originally and so these wonderful crispy spiced cheese thins are a perfect use for one of our local cheeses. Traditional wheels of farmhouse Leicester cheese are a much more crumbly, flavoursome affair than the better-known mass-produced red blocks offered in most supermarkets. Search out a good farm-made one for this recipe – it just might change your opinion of Red Leicester cheese, particularly if you thought it was miserably bland. That said, these work with other cheeses – try Stilton and fennel seeds or a hard goats' cheese and onion seed.

115 g (4 oz) butter, at room temperature
225 g (8 oz/1⅔ cups) grated Red Leicester, or other cheese
190 g (6 oz/1½ cups) plain (all-purpose) flour
pinch of salt
good pinch of chilli flakes or to taste
5 g (¼ oz) mild paprika

1. Line 2 baking sheets with baking paper.
2. Beat the butter and grated cheese together with a wooden spoon or electric whisk.
3. Add the remaining ingredients and then squeeze firmly together with your hands to form a well-mixed dough.
4. Roll into a 7 cm (4 in) diameter log, wrap in cling film (plastic wrap) and chill for at least 30 minutes. Preheat the oven to 200°C (400°F/Gas 6).
5. Slice the log as thinly as possible and place on the baking sheets. Bake for 10–12 minutes.
6. Store in an airtight container for up to a week. You can also freeze the uncooked log (or half of it) to slice and bake fresh another day.

WHAT THE TESTERS SAY

LYNSEY JONES AND HELEN WOOLDRIDGE – 'These tasted amazing and went down really well with friends – possibly the best recipe we tested!'

ROBINSON FAMILY – 'We all enjoyed them – I made one half of the batch with Red Leicester and chilli and the other half with Dolcelatte and fennel seeds.'

JOVANKA BJELIC – 'We loved them but go easy on the salt if using blue cheese and, also, I used chilli powder instead of flakes and it was too spicy, so add a little at a time and taste before you bake.'

TIP
YOU NEED TO CHILL THE DOUGH REALLY WELL SO YOU CAN SLICE IT PAPER THIN.

DIGESTIVE BISCUITS

PREPARATION	COOKING	MAKES	VEGETARIAN	NUT-FREE
15 mins	15 mins	30 small or 20 large biscuits		

I started making my own digestive biscuits when I lived in Sweden many moons ago. I doubt very much if I had been able to buy them I would ever have bothered trying to make them but having done so I am hooked on these. Try them and you just may never buy a packet from the supermarket again! See the finished biscuits on page 164.

125 g (4 oz/1 cup) plain (all-purpose) or wholemeal (whole wheat) flour
125 g (4 oz/1 cup) porridge (rolled) oats
10 g (½ oz) caster (superfine) sugar
5 g (¼ oz) baking powder
pinch of salt
75 g (2½ oz) butter
50 g (2 oz) milk

1. Preheat the oven to 190°C (375°F/Gas 5). Line 2 baking sheets with baking paper.
2. Put the porridge oats in a tall container and whizz with a hand blender until you have a flour-like consistency.
3. Mix all the dry ingredients together in a large bowl.
4. Rub in the butter using your fingers and thumbs until your mixture looks like fine breadcrumbs.
5. Stir in the milk – adding a little more milk if you need to make a soft but not sticky dough.
6. Roll out on a floured surface and cut into oblongs or rounds about 5 mm (¼ in) thick. Place on the prepared baking sheets.
7. Prick the tops if you wish, then bake for 15 minutes or until lightly browned.
8. Cool slightly then transfer to a wire rack to cool completely. Store in a sealed bag or airtight container for up to 2 weeks.

WHAT THE TESTERS SAY

RON SAWERS – 'I tried to cut rounds but it was hard work so I simply cut them into squares. I laid them on my cheeseboard for friends and they were blown away by my homemade cheese biscuits. So proud!'

RUTH HULME – 'I made these with a smaller amount of sugar for cheese and liked the crumbly texture.'

SAMUEL RAFTER – 'I love making my own version of something I can buy in the shops – it makes me smile. I added 100 g (3½ oz) sugar to make a sweet digestive and then coated one side thickly in Cadbury's chocolate – yum.'

TIP
ADD MORE SUGAR TO ENJOY THESE WITH A CUPPA RATHER THAN AS PART OF YOUR CHEESEBOARD.

OATCAKES

PREPARATION	COOKING	MAKES	VEGAN & VEGETARIAN	NUT-
20 mins	15–20 mins	about 20 biscuits (depending on size)	(unless you use lard!)	FREE

I got hooked on oatcakes when I worked in Sweden and have made them ever since. I use sunflower or olive oil depending on what end flavour I want but the other Lucy uses lard. I have to agree this wonderful pork fat is brilliant in the oatcakes and adds a really rounded flavour so the choice is yours. Here is the basic recipe, add whichever fat you like (use 75 g (2½ oz) hard fat, such as butter or lard in place of the oil, if you prefer) and then pop in herbs, seeds or spices to make the oatcakes your own. See the finished oatcakes on page 164.

280 g (10 oz/2¾ cups) porridge (rolled) oats
3 g (⅛ teaspoon) salt
75 g (2½ oz) sunflower oil
100 g (3½ oz) just boiled water

1. Preheat the oven to 190°C (375°F/Gas 5). Line a baking sheet with baking paper.
2. Put half the oats into a deep bowl and whizz with a hand blender, or put in a food processor and blend until you have a flour-like consistency.
3. Mix in the remaining oats, salt and the sunflower oil and work with your fingers and thumbs (if using hard fat rub in until the mixture resembles breadcrumbs).
4. Add the water and, using your hands, knead it to a soft dough and work into a ball. Leave it to stand for 10 minutes as this will help the dough solidify and it will be easier to roll.
5. Lay a large piece of cling film (plastic wrap) on a work surface and flatten half the dough out by hand roughly. Lay a second piece of cling film on top and roll the dough to 5 mm (¼ in) thick. Remove the top layer of cling film and either stamp into rounds using a pastry cutter or cut into oblongs, squares or triangles. You can even cut a large round using a plate as a template and then cut fan shaped pieces.
6. Lay them on the baking sheet and bake for 15–20 minutes or until just browned.
7. Cool on a wire rack and store in an airtight container for up to 3 weeks.

WHAT THE TESTERS SAY

JANET MEEKCOMS – 'I love the idea that by baking my own oatcakes I know what is in them and can vary it depending on what seeds, nuts and herbs I have about.'

LIZ EVERSON – 'They were really easy. Next time I would add some thyme or other herbs.'

BEN COLEBY – 'The dough seemed too wet to start but if you leave it for a few minutes it is easy to roll out. I added sunflower seeds but you need to chop them or you cannot roll the dough thin enough. I will add cardamom and fennel next time.'

TIP

THESE DO NOT HAVE TO BE PERFECTLY ROUND – YOU WANT THEM TO LOOK RUSTIC AND HOMEMADE – SO SQUARES OR OBLONGS ARE GREAT TOO.

TIP
YOU CAN MAKE THIS IN A SMALL, ROUND CAKE TIN AND CUT IT INTO WEDGES OR EVEN MAKE INDIVIDUAL ROUNDS IN RAMEKINS OR MUFFIN TINS.

FIG AND ALMOND SLAB FOR CHEESE (PAN DE HIGO)

PREPARATION 15 mins | **COOKING** 5 mins | **MAKES** 1 cheese loaf | **VEGETARIAN** | **GLUTEN-FREE** | **DAIRY-FREE**

This recipe is so simple – the most complicated bit of this is picking the stalks off the dried figs! It sums up Northern Spain for me but, in truth, I ate it first over the border in Biarritz, South West France. It is a dried slab of fruit and nuts, sweet and sticky and perfect with salty cheeses. So Roquefort from that part of France or Manchego, the mature white sheep's cheese from Spain are wonderful accompaniments. It is also easily packed up prettily for a gift.

200 g (7 oz/1⅓ cups) whole blanched almonds or a mixture of nuts
750 g (1lb 10 oz/4 cups) dried figs
100 g (3½ oz/generous ½ cup) dried apricots
50 g (2 oz) honey
pinch of ground cinnamon
slug of brandy (optional)

1. Preheat the oven to 200°C (400°F (Gas 6). Oil a 500 g (1 lb) loaf tin, then line with a double layer of cling film (plastic wrap).
2. Spread the nuts out on a shallow baking tray and bake for 5 minutes or until golden brown, remove and set aside to cool, then roughly chop, so some pieces are larger and some smaller.
3. Remove the stalks from the figs and put the fruit into a food processor with the apricots, honey and cinnamon and blend to a rough paste. Add a slug of brandy, if using, at this stage. This mix will be sticky and you might need to stop the processor and move the mix around to blend evenly.
4. Mix in the roughly chopped nuts.
5. Press the mixture into the prepared tin – you can use all the tin and have it flatter or pack into half the tin so it is full height.
6. Turn the shaped bar out onto a board covered in cling film (plastic wrap) and leave out in the open air in a cool place, such as a larder, for a week, lightly covered with paper towel or a clean cloth to protect it. Turn it to expose a different to edge to the air every couple of days. This will dry it out enough so that it can be sliced and then can be stored in the fridge, covered, for up to 6 months.

WHAT THE TESTERS SAY

COLIN MEEKCOMS – 'When Lucy asked me to try making this and I saw how easy it looked I agreed. I was blown away by how good it was with cheese – especially soft Brie and salty blue cheese. It keeps in the fridge for months so I only need to make a batch once in a blue moon and I am sorted.'

CLAIRE VAN DIJK – 'I adore this and I don't need cheese to eat it – great cut small with coffee after dinner.'

BEN COLEBY – 'I made and nibbled at it for days and it's great on a cheeseboard but also lovely as canapés – I served it wrapped in smoked ham – just make sure you toast the almonds well.'

Opposite, clockwise from the top: Oatcakes, Onion Seed and Garlic Thins, Fig and Almond Slab, Digestive Biscuits, Sesame Seed Crackers for Cheese

SESAME SEED CRACKERS FOR CHEESE

PREPARATION 10 mins | **COOKING** 10 mins | **MAKES** 30 crackers | **VEGAN & VEGETARIAN**

If you like sesame seeds you will love these. Baked to a dark colour they stay crispy and are great with cheese or pâté. Pack them in clear cellophane bags or as little boxes as perfect foodie gifts for friends. Experiment and add herbs and spices to vary the flavour. You need to use tiny seeds, so the dough can be rolled really thinly, hence why sesame are so good (and they have a real, nutty flavour). See the finished crackers on page 164.

150 g (5 oz/1 cup) sesame seeds
85 g (3 oz) vegetable oil
250 g (9 oz/1⅔ cups) wholemeal (whole wheat) flour
5 g (¼ oz) baking powder
8 g (⅓ oz) salt
80 g (3 oz) water

1. Preheat the oven to 200°C (400°F/Gas 6). Line 2 baking sheets with baking paper.
2. Put all the ingredients into a mixing bowl and stir together to a sticky dough. No kneading or serious mixing, you are just combining everything together. This will be far too wet and sticky to do anything with at this point.
3. Cover with cling film (plastic wrap) and set aside for at least 30 minutes – the dough will become firmer and more elastic.
4. Place half the dough on a large sheet of baking paper on the work surface, then lay cling film (plastic wrap) over the dough (I use 2 sheets slightly overlapping to give a wider piece). Roll the dough out through the cling film to less than 5 mm (¼ in) or as thin as the sesame seeds will allow then, using a round cutter or a knife, cut rounds, squares or oblongs of the mixture. Transfer, using a palette knife, to the prepared baking sheets. The dough will be strangely bendy and stretchy so may be difficult to move but ease a palette knife under the raw crackers and then invert it onto the baking sheet and they will plop down ready to bake.
5. Bake for 10 minutes or until they are well browned. Cool on a wire rack, then store in an airtight container for up to 1 month.

WHAT THE TESTERS SAY

RON SAWERS – 'I got into a bit of a mess not leaving the dough to stand – leave it and it will turn into something soft and easier to roll and you do need the baking paper and cling film.'

MARCELLA SCOTT – 'I was not sure I would bother to make a homemade cheese cracker when I can buy ones I like but I am a convert – these are great to simply snack on straight from the tin and I might add some spice next time.'

PENNY VICKERS – 'I love sesame seeds and the flavour. Cook them until dark golden brown or they are a bit bendy in texture – you want the baked crispy texture of the sesame seeds.'

TIP
YOU MUST BAKE THESE WELL OR THE TEXTURE WILL BE 'BENDY' RATHER THAN 'CRISPY'.

ONION SEED AND GARLIC THINS

PREPARATION	COOKING	MAKES	VEGAN &
10 mins	15 mins	about 30 thins	VEGETARIAN

A hybrid recipe that originated as a Swedish crispbread recipe years ago that went badly wrong. I like to make these long and thin to add some different shapes to my cheeseboard and they're great for dunking in hummus or other dips too. These need to be baked to a good brown colour so they're really crispy when cooled. Black onion seeds (also called kalonji or nigella seeds) are available from good supermarkets, Asian grocers and online. See the finished crackers on page 164.

160 g (5 oz/generous 1 cup) wholemeal (whole wheat) or rye flour
120 g (4 oz/1 cup) plain (all-purpose) flour
40 g (1½ oz) black onion seeds
40 g (1½ oz/¼ cup) sesame seeds
10 g (½ oz) bicarbonate of soda (baking soda)
5 g (1/4 oz) garlic granules
10 g (½ oz) salt
45 g (1½ oz) olive oil
175 g (6 oz) water

1. Put the flours and seeds into a bowl and add the bicarbonate of soda, garlic and salt. Stir well.
2. Add the olive oil and water and bring the soft dough together with your hands.
3. Turn out onto a floured surface and knead it all together for a few minutes. Cover and leave to rest for 10 minutes.
4. Preheat the oven to 200°C (400°F/Gas 6). Put the dough on a sheet of baking paper to stop it sticking to the surface and roll out as thinly as possible.
5. Cut into oblongs about 12 x 3 cm (5 x 1¼ in), transfer still on the paper to a baking sheet and bake for 15 minutes or until well browned and crispy. Cool on a wire rack and store in an airtight container for up to a month.

WHAT THE TESTERS SAY

IAN MEEKCOMS – 'As a cheese lover anything that can add to my cheeseboard always seems a good idea. Mine were all lengths and shapes but that is what made them great.'

BEN COLEBY – 'I just love the whole crispbread thing. I made these long and thin and they were excellent for dipping into homemade guacamole and salsa.'

LYDIA CUFFLIN AND SIMON CHILDS – 'These were a perfect thin crispbread to pile cheese on – I did not have onion seeds so used poppy seeds but still great.'

TIP
YOU CAN USE OTHER SEEDS IF YOU PREFER SUCH AS POPPY, SUNFLOWER OR CARAWAY SEEDS.

MINI SAVOURY SCONES

PREPARATION 15 mins | **COOKING** 10 mins | **MAKES** 30 mini scones | **VEGETARIAN** | **NUT-FREE**

We have been making mini savoury scones for years to host wonderful toppings for pre-dinner snacks and exotic canapés. These freeze well so bake a batch and take a few out when you need them for a pre-dinner bite. For perfect results, the dough should be wet and soft and handled as little as possible to give a light and easy rise.

15 g (½ oz) lemon juice (bottled is fine)
250 g (9 oz) milk
500 g (1 lb 2 oz) self-raising flour
5 g (¼ oz) baking powder
3 g (⅛ oz) dried dill or other herbs
100 g (3½ oz) butter
25 g (1 oz/¼ cup) grated Parmesan
good pinch of salt
1 egg

1. Preheat the oven to 220°C (430°F/Gas 7). Line a baking sheet with baking paper.
2. Add the lemon juice to the milk and set aside.
3. Put the flour, baking powder and herbs into a bowl and add the butter, cut into small pieces.
4. Rub the mixture between your fingers and thumbs until you get a mix that looks like fine breadcrumbs.
5. Add the cheese and salt and mix well.
6. Beat the egg into the milk and lemon juice and pour into the flour.
7. Bring it together using your hands – it should be a soft, slightly sticky dough – if it is firm, add a little more milk.
8. Turn onto a well-floured work surface and knead it briefly to bring it together but only just, then flatten out by hand to 2.5 cm (1 in) thick. Cut into little squares or 2.5 cm (1 in) diameter rounds using a mini pastry cutter, reshaping and cutting the trimmings as necessary.
9. Bake for 10 minutes until slightly browned and risen. Serve halved and topped as desired (see below).

SAVOURY TOPPINGS

TOMATOES AND ANCHOVY – mix 100 g (3½ oz) cream cheese with 5 g (¼ oz) tomato purée and 5 g (¼ oz) Worcestershire sauce. Add 3 anchovies, chopped. Pile onto the mini scones and top with more anchovy.

GRAVADLAX AND BEETROOT – grate 1 cooked, small beetroot and mix with 100 g (3½ oz) cream cheese and seasoning to taste. Top with a good slice of gravadlax or smoked salmon.

DRIED TOMATOES AND MOZZARELLA – tear off pieces of fresh mozzarella and place on the scones. Top with chopped bought or homemade dried tomato (see page 195) and drizzle with a little of the tomato oil, then add a caper or two if you like. Season well and pop into the oven at 200°C (400°F/Gas 6) for 5 minutes before serving.

STILTON AND CRANBERRY – blend 100 g (3½ oz) stilton with 100 g (3½ oz) plain yoghurt and pile on the scones. Top with a spoon of cranberry sauce.

WHAT THE TESTERS SAY

NAOMI HULME – 'I always keep some in a bag in the freezer – I don't add herbs or sweeten them but as a plain scone I can add sweet or savoury toppings any time.'

LYDIA CUFFLIN AND SIMON CHILDS – 'We made a batch every week during the ski season and they look fab piled high with different toppings.'

Opposite, from the top: Retro Olive Bakes, Mini Savoury Scones, Mini Marmite Bites

MINI MARMITE BITES

PREPARATION 5 mins | **COOKING** 8–10 mins | **MAKES** about 30 little thins | **VEGETARIAN** | **NUT-FREE**

What can I say? I am a Marmite lover – I always have been – and use Marmite in my cooking often, especially when I use cheese as it adds a punch. There are many little Marmite biscuit recipes out there – this one I developed from a little cheesy shortbread I made when we were young. You just get your hands into the bowl, squeeze it together and roll it into a log – what could be easier? A fabulous recipe to bake with children as they can simply squeeze and roll – perfect 'messy play' but the perfect grown-up biscuit too with a little glass of something!

100 g (3½ oz/generous ¾ cup) finely grated cheese
20 g (¾ oz) Marmite
175 g (6 oz/scant 1½ cups) self-raising flour
100 g (3½ oz) butter, at room temperature
pinch of coarsely ground black pepper

1. Line 2 baking sheets with baking paper. Put all the ingredients into a bowl and literally squeeze it all together using your hands until you have a stiff dough.
2. Turn out onto a clean work surface and make into 2 logs about 3 cm (1¼ in) in diameter.
3. Wrap in cling film (plastic wrap) and chill the logs for 30 minutes. Preheat the oven to 190°C (375°F/Gas 5).
4. Slice into 5 mm (¼ in) discs and place on the prepared baking sheets.
5. Bake for 8–10 minutes or until golden brown.
6. Cool slightly, then transfer to a wire rack to cool completely. Store in an airtight container. The mixture can be frozen, then removed from the freezer 15 minutes before slicing and baking.

WHAT THE TESTERS SAY

MAURICE FLYNN – 'I am not a Marmite fan but the neighbour's children loved them. I actually crumbled the ingredients together before squeezing it to incorporate the mix – easy recipe.'

GEMMA HEDGES – 'I made these as nibbles for pre-Sunday lunch and made them while we were cooking the meal. My little niece did most of the mixing – easy, fun and I LOVE THEM.'

LYDIA CUFFLIN AND SIMON CHILDS – 'These are just baked and we are on our way to eating them all from the baking sheets with a glass of wine – ridiculously good.'

TIP

TRY USING RYE FLOUR FOR A MORE RUSTIC FLAVOUR AND TEXTURE.

RETRO OLIVE BAKES

PREPARATION	COOKING	MAKES	VEGETARIAN	NUT-FREE
15 mins + freezing	15–20 mins	40		

Back in the mists of time when olives were terribly sophisticated – yes, I'm talking about the 1970s – the other Lucy's mum went to America for a holiday and returned with some recipes, including a version of this made then with pimento-stuffed olives. They've been a favourite in her family ever since. Now, in more cosmopolitan times, we have all sorts of olives to choose from stuffed with all manner of delicious titbits – current favourites of ours would have to be those stuffed with anchovy but the choice is yours.

115 g (4 oz) butter, at room temperature
110 g (3½ oz/generous 1 cup) Parmesan or pecorino, finely grated
110 g (3½ oz/generous ¾ cup) finely grated Cheddar
150 g (5 oz/1¼ cups) plain (all-purpose) flour
pinch of paprika
pinch of ground cumin, optional
40 g (1½ oz) pitted or stuffed green olives

1. Line a baking sheet with baking paper.
2. Cream together the butter and cheeses until smooth.
3. Mix in the flour and spices. Cover the bowl and chill for at least 1 hour.
4. Dry the olives on paper towels. Using wet hands, take a ball of cheese mixture close in size to the olives and flatten it in your palm. Work the mixture up around the olive, and then very gently roll it around between your palms. Make sure the cheese mixture completely seals in the olive, so you have a ball of mixture with an olive hidden inside.
5. Place on the baking sheet and freeze for 15 minutes or until needed. (They can be frozen ahead of time and cooked from frozen the day you want to serve them, so they are a great idea for entertaining when time is short as you can have these made ahead to this point.) Meanwhile, preheat the oven to 220°C (430°F/Gas 7).
6. Cook from frozen for 20 minutes or until golden and the pastry is no longer doughy. Allow to cool slightly before serving as they will firm up, but you can let them go cold and warm through for 5 minutes just before serving if more convenient.

WHAT THE TESTERS SAY

HATTIE CUFFLIN – 'Surprisingly easy to knock up and so good we ate them all off the baking tray – I used plain stoned green olives but would try another sort next time.'

NAOMI AND RUTH HULME – 'They are fantastic. We shared them with friends over a glass of wine and we ate the lot!'

JACQUI MELVILLE AND SUZANNE QUINTNER – ''70s retro – absolutely! It is hard not to eat them all before the guests arrive!'

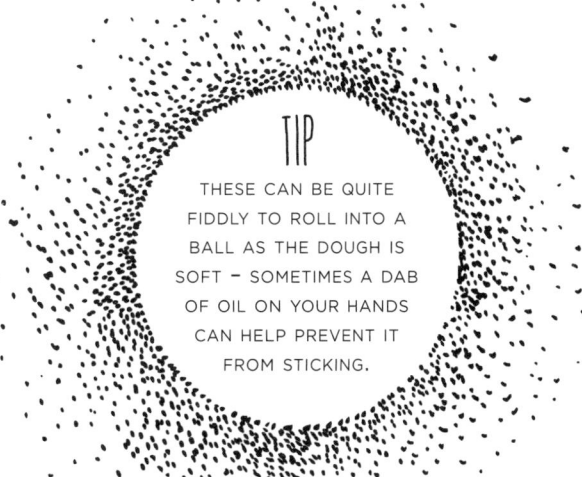

TIP

THESE CAN BE QUITE FIDDLY TO ROLL INTO A BALL AS THE DOUGH IS SOFT – SOMETIMES A DAB OF OIL ON YOUR HANDS CAN HELP PREVENT IT FROM STICKING.

CHRISTMAS IS A TIME OF GATHERINGS, PARTIES AND SOCIALISING, SEEING FRIENDS AND FAMILY AND WHAT COULD BE BETTER THAN HAVING SOMETHING HOMEMADE TO SHARE WITH EVERYONE?

THIS CHAPTER INCLUDES A STEP-BY-STEP GUIDE ON HOW TO MARZIPAN, ICE AND DECORATE THAT ALL IMPORTANT CHRISTMAS CAKE AND SOME IDEAS TO GIVE YOUR FAVOURITE YEAR ROUND RECIPES A FESTIVE TWIST.

HOMEMADE TREATS CAN MAKE WONDERFUL GIFTS SO PLAN AHEAD, BAKE AND MAKE, WRAP AND RIBBON AND ENJOY THE FESTIVE SEASON.

FESTIVE TREATS

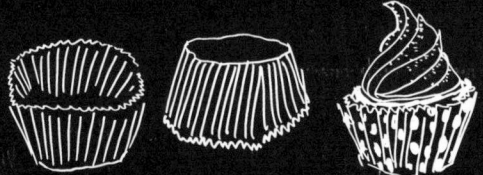

CHESTNUT CUPS

PREPARATION	COOKING	MAKES	VEGETARIAN	GLUTEN-FREE
15 mins + chilling	none (except melting)	20 petit fours-sized cups		

Chestnuts say 'Christmas' to me and in this recipe of Lucy LT's we have used them in their simplest form, ready-cooked! The easiest to use here is canned, ready sweetened purée but if not available you can buy unsweetened purée or whole, cooked chestnuts and purée them yourself, then sweeten the purée to taste. These decadent little treats are gorgeous whichever chestnuts you use and once you have the hang of the cups you can fill them with other fillings at different times of the year. Try the berry buttercream on page 197 or ganache on page 196, left to set enough to pipe.

300 g (10½ oz) dark chocolate
200 g (7 oz) sweetened chestnut purée
200 g (7 oz) double (heavy) cream
dash of liqueur (optional)

1. Place 20 mini (petit four) cake cases on a baking tray.
2. Melt the chocolate in a bowl over a saucepan of gently simmering water and when it is melted remove it from the heat. Transfer 100 g (3½ oz) to a small bowl and set aside to cool but not set again.
3. Dip a pastry brush in the remaining chocolate, brush a light film on the inside of the paper case, invert them and leave to set. Chill the cases then repeat so you have a double layer of chocolate.
4. Meanwhile whisk the sweetened chestnut purée with the cream (and liqueure if using) until thick, then add the reserved 100 g (3½ oz) cooled melted chocolate.
5. When the chocolate cups are solid, remove the cases if you wish and then pipe or spoon the chestnut cream into them.
6. Store for up to 3 days in the fridge.

WHAT THE TESTERS SAY

SIMON EBBS – 'I was worried that they might not look right as my chocolate cup edges seemed a bit uneven, but piping in the filling covered up the rough bits and made them look really professional. I was very proud of the end result.'

LYDIA CUFFLIN AND SIMON CHILDS – 'Painting the chocolate in the little cases was easier than I thought it would be, but Lucy suggested we used stiffer foil cases – a good tip.'

MANDY FISHER – 'These definitely have the wow factor. I decorated mine with some big, soft silver and gold sugar balls that I found in the supermarket but you could fill the cases with all sorts of fruity or nutty stuff if you don't like chestnuts.'

TIP — THIS CHESTNUT CREAM ALSO MAKES A FABULOUS CAKE FILLING.

FESTIVE TREATS

JEWELLED BISCOTTI

PREPARATION 10 mins + cooling time

COOKING 40–45 mins

MAKES about 60 thin-cut biscotti

VEGETARIAN

*The word biscotti literally means twice cooked in Italian (*bi = two *and* cotti = cook*) and is the origin of our word 'biscuit'. Daisy, one of our most creative chalet hosts at Skiworld, introduced me to the simplicity of biscotti-making many years ago. This recipe is foolproof and very adaptable. Here we have given them a festive makeover – great to serve with puds, dunked in coffee or bagged up as gifts – they last over 1 month once baked so make ahead! If you prefer large, dunking biscotti, cut about 30 thicker ones and second-bake for 30 minutes to dry them out.*

100 g (3½ oz) mixed coloured glacé cherries
250 g (9 oz/2 cups) plain (all-purpose) flour
10 g (½ oz) baking powder
200 g (7 oz/scant 1 cup) caster (superfine) sugar
Finely grated zest of 2 oranges, plus the juice of 1 orange
3 g (⅛ oz) ground cinnamon
150 g (5 oz/generous 1 cup) hazelnuts, chopped
2 eggs

1. Preheat the oven to 180°C (350°F/Gas 4). Line a baking sheet with baking paper.
2. Chop the glacé cherries finely and put into a bowl with all of the other ingredients. Mix together with a spoon or your hands until you have a soft dough.
3. Divide the mixture in half and form into soft logs (wet hands might help here) and place them side by side on the baking sheet – do not flatten as this will happen during cooking.
4. Bake for 25 minutes until risen and dark golden brown. It is important to leave this to get completely cold before slicing – it's best left overnight. You can bake up to this point and freeze this log and bake again another day.
5. Once cold and ready to second-bake, preheat the oven to 150°C (300°F/Gas 2). Use a large bread knife and slice the logs very thinly – you should get about 30 from each log – and lay them onto baking sheets lined with baking paper.
6. Cook again for 15–20 minutes or until the biscotti are only just golden brown – do not overcook them – you are really drying them out here.

WHAT THE TESTERS SAY

ELLA AND ANTONIA ARGENTIER – 'These are fat-free so biscotti with coffee is a firm favourite of ours. We make them all year round but add nuts and cinnamon only.'

CLAIRE VAN DIJK – 'These make brilliant Christmas gifts – I bought some cellophane bags on the internet and tied them up with ribbons.'

RUTH HULME – 'These are so easy to make – I never thought about making a Christmas version but I love them.'

TIP

TRY LEMON ZEST INSTEAD OF ORANGE AND DRIED BERRIES AND PUMPKIN SEEDS IN PLACE OF THE GLACÉ CHERRIES.

MINCEMEAT TWIGS

PREPARATION 10 mins | **COOKING** 15 mins | **MAKES** 10 twigs | **DAIRY-FREE**

When chalet catering over the Christmas period we are always looking for simple treats for Christmas, and these were created on a day when we had planned to make some little tartlets, but found ourselves without a suitable tin! You can serve them warm or cold for dessert with brandy butter (simply beat some softened butter with twice its quantity of icing sugar and beat in some brandy to taste) or whipped cream, or as a little treat with coffee or a cuppa throughout the festive season.

1 packet of 10 sheets of filo pastry
½ x 411 g (14 oz) jar of good mincemeat
icing (confectioners') sugar, for dusting

1. Preheat the oven to 200°C (400°F/Gas 6). Line a baking sheet with baking paper.
2. Lay a sheet of filo pastry onto a clean work surface, making sure the remaining sheets are covered or they will dry out while you are working.
3. You are going to lay a narrow strip of mincemeat on the filo across the shorter width of the pastry. Spoon 2 teaspoons of mincemeat onto the pastry at one short end, 2 cm (¾ in) in from the edge, and drag it in a thin line, no wider than the width of the dried fruit in the mincemeat, from one side to the other across the pastry, stopping 2 cm (¾ in) before you reach the other edge.
4. Fold the ends over and then roll as tightly as you can so you have a long, thin twig-shaped filo parcel with the mincemeat trapped inside. Transfer to the prepared baking sheet and repeat with the other filo sheets and mincemeat.
5. Dust very generously with icing sugar and bake for 15 minutes or until the filo is crispy and golden and the sugar browned. Transfer to a wire rack to cool. Dust with more icing sugar to serve.

WHAT THE TESTERS SAY

LIZ EVERSON – 'Found them a bit fiddly but once they were baked I realised the important thing is that there are no holes in the pastry. Other than that they do not need to be neat at all – in fact the rougher the better.'

NAOMI HULME – 'This was a great chalet extra for after-dinner around Christmas time. The guests loved them and you only need a few spoons of mincemeat to make enough for 10, so a great way to use up a bit of mincemeat at the bottom of a jar.'

BEN COLEBY – 'I thought these were fantastic – be generous with the sugar before baking to make them really crispy. And they're best warmed just before serving.'

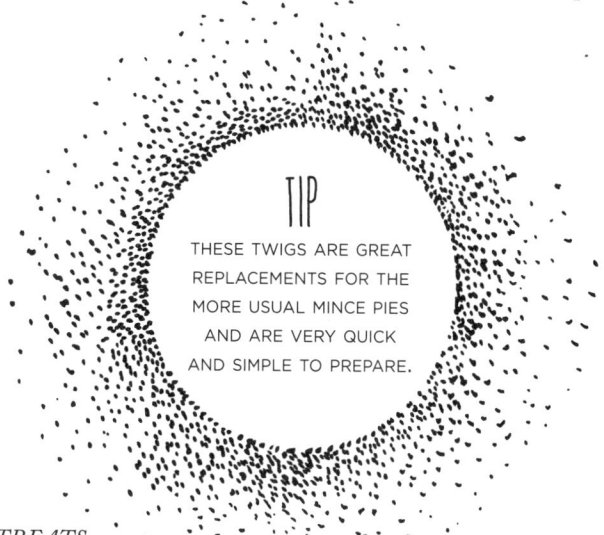

TIP
THESE TWIGS ARE GREAT REPLACEMENTS FOR THE MORE USUAL MINCE PIES AND ARE VERY QUICK AND SIMPLE TO PREPARE.

FESTIVE TREATS

PLUMP FRUIT CAKE

PREPARATION 20 mins | **COOKING** 2–2 ½ hours | **MAKES** 1 x 25 cm (10 in) cake | **VEGETARIAN** | **NUT-FREE**

Both of us Lucys love fruit cake and both of us have our favourite fast or boiled fruit cake recipe. Which to share with you was the question? So we had a bake off – mine was delicious, although I say it myself, but I had to concede. This recipe, that the other Lucy has been making for years, is simply stunning. Kept for a day it tastes like it has matured over months, is dense with fruit and packed with flavour. Made in one saucepan with no fuss, it is perfect to decorate as your Christmas cake. Use fruit cake mix or any dried fruit – it's a great opportunity to use up oddments from your store cupboard.

80 g (3 oz) golden (corn) syrup
80 g (3 oz) black treacle (molasses)
50 g (2 oz) strong-flavoured clear honey
250 g (9 oz/1¼ cups) soft dark brown sugar
200 g (7 oz) double (heavy) cream
7 g (¼ oz) mixed spice
250 g (9 oz) butter, at room temperature
grated zest of 1 orange
grated zest of 1 lemon
6 eggs
400 g (14 oz) chopped prunes
100 g (3½ oz) mixed dried fruit
500 g (1 lb 2 oz/4 cups) plain (all-purpose) flour
3 g (⅛ oz) bicarbonate of soda (baking soda)
brandy, to taste

1. Preheat the oven to 180°C (350°F/Gas 4). Line a 25 cm (10 in) round, deep cake tin with baking paper.
2. Gently heat the syrup, treacle, honey, sugar, cream and spice in a saucepan, stirring occasionally, and bring to the boil. Allow to cool slightly, then add the butter, a knob at a time, and stir until melted. Add the orange and lemon zest.
3. Add the eggs, beat until combined, then add the fruit and mix well.
4. Sift in the flour and bicarbonate of soda and stir until evenly mixed. Spoon into the tin and bake for about 2–2½ hours, or until a skewer inserted comes out clean. Dribble over a few spoonfuls of brandy and leave to cool in the tin.
5. When cold, generously dribble with more spoonfuls of brandy, remove from the tin and wrap well in foil (leaving the cake in the baking paper). If icing the cake, leave for 5 days before icing (giving it a couple more feeds of brandy, if desired). It will keep for a good few weeks in an airtight container.

WHAT THE TESTERS SAY

IAN COLEBY – 'Just lots of weighing out – the rest was easy and it has kept really well wrapped in foil in a tin for 3 months.'

JO CURD – 'Friends loved it when I made it for a group get together – I didn't ice it as it looked lovely as it was.'

JANET MEEKCOMS – 'I have made many fruit cakes and this is one of the best ever – it is so easy and tastes mature on the first day. I loved the fact I could use up what dried fruit I had in my cupboard.'

TIP
THIS IS A BIG CAKE FOR A CELEBRATION BUT YOU CAN HALVE THE QUANTITIES AND MAKE A 20 CM (8 IN) CAKE (REDUCE THE COOKING TIME TO ABOUT 1½ HOURS).

| VEGETARIAN | NUT-FREE |

CHRISTMAS PUDDING BROWNIES

PREPARATION	COOKING	MAKES
10 mins	30 mins	12 squares

This recipe is a winner with children, grown-ups, Christmas pudding lovers and haters alike. Keep these in an airtight container for over the festive season or serve warm with ice cream for Christmas dinner – they will be a huge success.

1 Make Lucy's Chewy Chocolate Brownies (see page 122) but omit the white chocolate.
2 When you have put the brownie mix into the tin, crumble 250 g (9 oz) Christmas pudding evenly over the surface (you can use a bought one or leftover if you have some).
3 Bake for 30 minutes, then cut and store as before.

WHAT THE TESTERS SAY

JOVANKA BJELIC – 'These are fantastic. My family are not Christmas pud lovers but everyone ate these and asked for more.'

ELLA ARGENTIER – 'My mum is English and my Dad is French and we live in France, so at Christmas we do some English things and this recipe is perfect for my French friends to try Christmas pud – I would make these again.'

RON SAWERS – 'We have a houseful every Christmas and this is a great way of serving Christmas pudding and all its lovely flavours to those who think they do not like it – a winner.'

| VEGETARIAN | GLUTEN-FREE |

CHRISTMAS FLAPJACK

PREPARATION	COOKING	MAKES
20 mins	15–20 mins	16 bars

Flapjack can be ordinary but not if you load it up with festive flavours as here.

1 Follow the Honey and Lavender Flapjack recipe on page 125. Omit the lavender and add the grated zest of 1 orange, 50 g (2 oz) dried cranberries, 50 g (2 oz/½ cup) pecans or walnuts, chopped, 7 g (¼ oz) ground cinnamon and 50 g (2 oz) chopped crystallised ginger.
2 Bake as in the original recipe.

WHAT THE TESTERS SAY

CLAIRE VAN DIJK – 'Once this is baking the smell of Christmas will fill your kitchen.'

COLIN MEEKCOMS – 'I am a complete novice and I did not line my tin on my first batch – mistake! The second batch I lined it – success. So even if you've never baked, you can do these.'

RUTH HULME – 'I am now inspired to try a Christmas twist to all my favourite cakes and cookie recipes.'

HOW TO MARZIPAN AND FLAT-ICE A RICH FRUIT CAKE

Lucy LT shares her expertise: you need to get the basics right. To use an analogy – if you don't wear the right underwear it doesn't matter how fantastic the outfit is, you'll still have lumps and bumps where you don't want them. The same goes when you marzipan and flat-ice a cake!

HANDY TIPS

- For a neat rim to your cake, make sure the baking paper is pushed right into the corners of the tin.

- For the glaze, sieve 120 g (4 oz) of apricot jam into a small saucepan, add 15 g (½ oz) water and bring to the boil.

- Put the marzipaned cake onto an upside-down cake tin or saucepan – it's much easier to ice off the board.

- Keep your equipment and work surface completely dry when rolling out on icing sugar. You can also use cornflour – it's less sticky than icing sugar, but brush off any excess as it is not pleasant to eat.

- For clean and sharp edges to the marzipan and icing, keep the blade of the knife clean and dry.

- For a taller-looking cake, put the cake on a thick cake board of the same diameter, then marzipan and ice over this. (Also useful if you are stacking cakes.)

- Use different sized and coloured boards stacked up to create interesting bases for your cake.

- If using ribbon to tie round your cake, use the same ribbon around the edges of the cake board to carry your colour scheme through to the base.

- If it's a celebration, decorate your knife with ribbon to match the cake.

WHAT YOU'LL NEED

- knife with a long blade (such as a bread knife)
- tin the cake was cooked in
- cake board 5 cm (2 in) larger than the cake if you want to feature the board, or 2.5 cm (1 in) larger (to allow for the marzipan and icing) if you want it to be almost concealed (when stacking for instance)
- string
- apricot jam
- small saucepan
- pastry brush
- 1 kg (2lb 3 oz) marzipan (almond paste)
- 1 kg (2lb 3 oz) ready-to-roll icing (fondant)
- icing (confectioners') sugar or cornflour (cornstarch), for dusting

Marzipan and Flat-Ice a Rich Fruit Cake Step-by-Step

1. IF THE CAKE IS NOT FLAT ON TOP, PUT IT BACK INTO ITS TIN. WITH A LONG KNIFE AND A GENTLE SAWING MOTION, USE THE TIN AS A GUIDE TO LEVEL OFF THE CAKE.

2. TAKE THE CAKE OUT THE TIN AND PLACE ON A CAKE BOARD ON AN UPTURNED TIN. MEASURE THE CAKE CIRCUMFERENCE AND DIAMETER WITH A PIECE OF STRING AND PUT KNOTS IN IT TO MARK THE SIZE.

3. USING THE KNOTTED STRING AS YOUR GUIDE, ROLL THE MARZIPAN TO JUST LONGER THAN THE REQUIRED LENGTH AND A LITTLE WIDER THAN CAKE HEIGHT. FOR EASE, USE 2 SHORTER LENGTHS AND HALF THE CIRCUMFERENCE EACH WHEN ROLLED.

4. BRUSH THE SIDES OF THE CAKE WITH HOT APRICOT GLAZE. TRIM THE MARZIPAN STRIPS SO THEY HAVE STRAIGHT EDGES THEN GENTLY ROLL THEM UP.

5. PRESS THE END OF ONE MARZIPAN STRIP ONTO THE CAKE AND UNROLL, GENTLY FLATTENING IT ONTO THE CAKE. DO THE SAME WITH THE OTHER. TRIM THE ENDS WHERE THEY MEET.

6. WITH A GENTLE SAWING MOTION, TRIM OFF THE TOP OF THE EXCESS MARZIPAN. COVER THE TOP OF THE CAKE IN THE SAME WAY, REMBERING TO BRUSH THE CAKE SURFACE WITH HOT APRICOT GLAZE BEFORE COVERING WITH THE MARZIPAN.

7 REMOVE THE CAKE BOARD FROM UNDER THE CAKE SO THAT IT LIES FLAT ON THE UPTURNED CAKE TIN. USING A PIECE OF STRING, MEASURE THE CAKE FROM THE BASE OF ONE SIDE TO THE OTHER

8 USING THE STRING AS YOUR GUIDE, ROLL OUT ICING A LITTLE LARGER THAN NEEDED. LIGHTLY BRUSH THE MARZIPAN WITH BOILED WATER TO HELP IT STICK, AND USING YOUR ROLLING PIN TO LIFT, DRAPE THE ICING OVER THE CAKE.

9 WITH DRY HANDS DUSTED WITH ICING SUGAR, EASE THE ICING ONTO THE SIDES OF THE CAKE, SMOOTHING AS YOU GO. TAKE CARE NOT TO PULL IT TOO MUCH AS YOU DON'T WANT TO TEAR IT.

10 LIGHTLY 'POLISH' THE SURFACE USING SMALL, CIRCULAR MOTIONS WITH WELL DUSTED HANDS ALL OVER THE TOP AND DOWN THE SIDES. GENTLY EASE THE ICING IN AT THE BASE SO IT STICKS EVENLY TO THE SIDES.

11 TRIM THE EXCESS ALL ROUND THE BASE OF THE CAKE USING A SHARP KNIFE. GENTLY POLISH AGAIN TO MAKE SURE EVERYTHING IS EVENLY SMOOTH AND ADHERED TO THE MARZIPAN.

12 TRANSFER TO THE CAKE BOARD AND COVER WITH A CLEAN TEA (DISH) TOWEL. IDEALLY, IF THERE'S TIME, LEAVE IT FOR 24 HOURS FOR THE ICING TO FIRM UP BEFORE ADDING YOUR FINAL DECORATIONS. WHEN DECORATED, STORE IN AN UPSIDE-DOWN, AIRTIGHT CONTAINER.

FESTIVE CAKE DECORATING

Cake decorating has moved on from the stiff and slightly formal icing confections of a few years ago – just put 'cake decorating' into an internet search and you can spend hours (days, even) marvelling at the sheer variety of shapes, colours and designs. They can still be fantastic works of art but cakes are now more about fun, creativity and flair rather than proficiency with the piping bag. Supermarkets now carry a great range of cake decorating accessories and, if you haven't a cake decorating shop locally, the internet can provide you with more colours and flavours than you could shake a rolling pin at. The confectionery aisle is also a great place to find fun – and often edible – trimmings. These cakes are the other lucy's creative work – they're ingenious!

- THIS EASY-TO-ACHIEVE CHRISTMAS CAKE USES 3 DIFFERENT-SIZED BOARDS TO ADD HEIGHT AND COLOUR.

- THE LITTLE RED GIFT BOXES ARE RE-USED CHRISTMAS TREE DECORATIONS WITH THE STRING LOOPS CUT OFF.

- STICK THE BOXES TOGETHER WITH DABS OF GLUE AND REST ON A DISC OF GREEN FONDANT ICING. THIS ADDS COLOUR AND WILL ALSO PROTECT THE EDIBLE ICING FROM ANY BITS OF GLITTER THAT MAY COME OFF THE DECORATIONS.

- SIT THE DISC OF FONDANT ITSELF ON A SAME-SIZED DISC OF BAKING PAPER SO THAT THE DECORATION IS EASILY REMOVED AND RE-SITED WHEN CUTTING THE CAKE.

- PLACE SOME RED BEAD ROPE (MINE WAS AN OLD GARLAND FROM THE CHRISTMAS TREE) AROUND THE BOTTOM OF THE CAKE AND SECURE WITH A DAB OF ROYAL ICING.

JUST A QUICK SAFETY NOTE: IT MAY BE TEMPTING TO STICK DRESS-MAKING PINS INTO CAKES TO FIX RIBBONS ETC., BUT DON'T AS SOMEONE MIGHT SWALLOW ONE BY MISTAKE. PINS CAN BE PUSHED INTO THE CAKE BOARD, BUT ONLY 'FOOD GRADE' BITS – COCKTAIL STICKS OR CAKE DOWELLING – SHOULD BE USED FOR FIXING DECORATIONS TO THE CAKE ITSELF. A LITTLE BLOB OF ROYAL ICING IS OFTEN A GOOD OPTION.

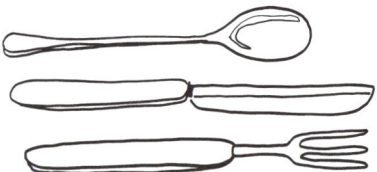

- THIS SIMPLE BUT EFFECTIVE CHRISTMAS CAKE AGAIN USES THE THREE DIFFERENT-SIZED BOARDS.

- THE LITTLE CHRISTMAS TREE CAME IN A PACK OF FOUR AND WAS BOUGHT IN A SUPERMARKET. (WE'VE USED A NUMBER OF LITTLE TREES IN DIFFERENT COLOURS ON A LARGER CAKE AND IT LOOKED WONDERFUL.)

- PUSH THE TREE INTO A DISC OF FONDANT ICING TO PROTECT THE CAKE FROM GLITTER AND TO GIVE THE TREE A STABLE BASE ON WHICH TO SIT.

- WRAP A LARGE PEARL ROPE (FROM A HABERDASHERY DEPARTMENT) AROUND THE BASE OF THE CAKE AND AROUND THE BASE OF THE TREE (IT IS ALSO PERFECT FOR WEDDING AND CHRISTENING CAKES). GLUE 2 OF THE 'PEARLS' TO THE TOP OF THE TREE.

- THIS ELEGANT DECORATION SHOWS JUST HOW EASY IT CAN BE TO CREATE A TRULY ORIGINAL CHRISTMAS CAKE.

- SIT THE CAKE ON 2 BOARDS OF DIFFERENT SIZES BUT OF THE SAME COLOUR.

- SIMPLY BEND AND SHAPE A METAL AND PEARL MISTLETOE SPRIG TO PARTIALLY CAGE THE PLAINLY ICED CAKE. (I FOUND THIS ONE IN A POP-UP, SEASONAL SHOP OR YOU MAY FIND SOMETHING SIMILAR IN A POUND SHOP AT CHRISTMAS TIME).

- THIS CHRISTMAS CAKE HAS THE WOW FACTOR BUT IS A DODDLE TO ACHIEVE.

- SIT THE CAKE ON 2 SILVER CAKE BOARDS. USE DOUBLE-SIDED RIBBON WITH A VERY THIN WIRE IN ITS EDGES AS IT IS SO EASY TO TIE ROUND AND CREATE THE PERFECT BOW (AVAILABLE IN HABERDASHERY DEPARTMENTS).

- THE DECORATION ON THE TOP IS THE TOP OFF AN OLD BUT FUNKY CHRISTMAS TREE STAR WHICH HAD COME APART FROM THE BIT THAT FIXED IT TO THE TREE (SIMILAR DECORATIONS ARE ALWAYS AROUND DURING THE FESTIVE SEASON).

- THIS CAKE HAS THE PERFECT DECORATION FOR CHRISTMAS BUT IS ALSO MORE THAN SUITABLE FOR WEDDING ANNIVERSARIES AND OTHER SPECIAL OCCASIONS.

- TIE GILDED PEARS (FROM A DEPARTMENT STORE) TOGETHER WITH CRÊPE PAPER RIBBON AND FINISH IN A BOW. SECURE IN PLACE WITH BLOBS OF ROYAL ICING OR COCKTAIL STICKS.

- USE PEARL ROPE TO ENCIRCLE THE SMALLER OF THE 2 CAKE BOARDS.

- AROUND THE BOTTOM OF THE CAKE USE THE SAME PAPER RIBBON.

Sweet or savoury, whether you dip, coat or smother it – most baking loves a topping.

Add a touch of love to your cake and fill it with your own fast 10-minute jam or smother your foccacia with home-dried tomatoes. Make balsamic syrup that will linger on your tastebuds and add toppings to cakes that will turn them into something truly heavenly. The recipes are here.

There is, after all, a reason why we have the saying 'it is the icing on the cake' – it is the bit that makes all the difference!

See page 8 for a few foolproof tips before you start.

TOPPINGS AND FILLINGS

| VEGAN & VEGETARIAN | GLUTEN-FREE | NUT-FREE | DAIRY-FREE |

10-Minute Berry Jam

PREPARATION 5 mins | **COOKING** 10 mins | **MAKES** 5–6 jars

Place **900 g (2 lb) frozen raspberries** and **700 g (1 lb 9 oz/generous 3 cups) jam sugar (with added pectin)** into a large saucepan and heat gently, until the fruit defrosts and the sugar dissolves. Then bring to the boil and boil for 5 minutes only. Let it rest for a few minutes as this will help the fruit stay suspended in the jam and not float to the top of the jar. Pot into sterilised jars, label and store in a dark cupboard for up to 1 year.

ALTERNATIVES

ORANGE AND RASPBERRY – add the grated zest of an orange to the basic recipe.
BLUEBERRY AND VANILLA – use frozen blueberries and add 10 g (½ oz) vanilla extract.
BERRY AND CHILLI – use frozen mixed berries and add a pinch (or to taste) of chilli flakes.
INTENSE STRAWBERRY – use frozen strawberries and a good grinding of black pepper.
BERRY AND GINGER – add a teaspoon or two of ground (or some chopped crystallised) ginger to any berry jam.

| VEGETARIAN | GLUTEN-FREE | NUT-FREE |

Foolproof Lemon Curd

PREPARATION 5 mins | **COOKING** 10 mins | **MAKES** 2 jars

Beat **200 g (7 oz/generous ¾ cup) caster (superfine) sugar** with **100 g (3½ oz) butter**, at room temperature, until pale and fluffy, then beat in **3 eggs**, one at a time, then **1 extra egg yolk**. Add the finely grated zest and juice of **4 lemons**. Don't panic now as it may well curdle – it does not matter. Pour the mixture into a saucepan and slowly cook over a medium heat, stirring all the time, for about 10 minutes until thickened, smooth and glossy and the curd sticks to the back of the wooden spoon. Don't let it boil. Pot in sterilised jars and store in the fridge for a month or freeze it.

TIP
LEMON CURD ADDED TO BUTTERCREAM MAKES A FABULOUS CUPCAKE TOPPING.

| VEGAN & VEGETARIAN | GLUTEN-FREE | NUT-FREE | DAIRY-FREE |

FAST BALSAMIC SYRUP

PREPARATION 2 mins | **COOKING** 2–6 mins | **MAKES** 2 litres

Place **800 g (1¾ lb) balsamic vinegar**, **1 kg (2 lb 3 oz/4½ cups) jam sugar (with pectin)**, **6 g (¼ oz) salt**, **250 g (9 oz) water**, **2 large garlic cloves, finely grated**, and **5 g (¼ oz) dried thyme** in a saucepan. Heat slowly, stirring, to dissolve the sugar. Bring to the boil and boil for 4–5 minutes. Sieve and bottle while still hot (use the sterilised vinegar bottle and other sterilised bottles). This will keep in a dark cupboard for up to 1 year. Great for dipping bread, drizzling over hot steaks or in dressings and marinades.

ALTERNATIVES

LAVENDER – omit the garlic and thyme and add 10 g (½ oz) dried lavender flowers. Wonderful drizzled over strawberries.

FENNEL – add the garlic and substitute 5 g (¼ oz) fennel seeds, lightly crushed, for the thyme. Excellent drizzled over fish.

JUNIPER AND GIN – add the garlic and substitute 5 g (¼ oz) juniper berries, lightly crushed, for the thyme. Add a slug of gin just before bottling. Good with hot pork and drizzled over salad with pâtés.

| VEGAN & VEGETARIAN | GLUTEN-FREE | NUT-FREE | DAIRY-FREE |

PRESERVED LEMONS

PREPARATION 5 mins + marinating | **COOKING** none | **MAKES** 1 large jar

For each large jar, wash and quarter **3–4 large lemons**, packing them in so it is half-full. Spoon in **20 g (¾ oz) coarse sea salt** and then fill the jar with the remaining lemon quarters, making sure they stand a little proud of the rim. Add a further **20 g (¾ oz) salt** and then push the lid down and screw it on firmly. Leave it at room temperature for 4 days, inverting then righting the jar each day so the salt and juices mingle. Place in the fridge. They are ready in 2 weeks but will keep for over 6 months.

To use: chop and deseed a lemon quarter. Add to game, beef or lamb stews or tagines about 10 minutes before the end of cooking. Add to cookie dough or shortbread, use the juice in dressings or sauté with chicken livers.

OVEN-DRIED TOMATOES IN GARLIC OIL

PREPARATION	COOKING	MAKES	VEGAN &	GLUTEN-	NUT-FREE	DAIRY-
10 mins	overnight	1 jar	VEGETARIAN	FREE		FREE

Having discovered the love for homemade bread you need to top it off with something it deserves, and these oven-dried tomatoes are fabulous. They are also a great way to serve winter tomatoes, which can lack flavour. Fill your oven and pack them into jars as they will last months.

6–7 ripe tomatoes
100 g (3½ oz) olive oil
1 garlic clove, finely grated
salt and pepper
1 tablespoon capers (optional)

1. Preheat the oven to 120°C (250°F/Gas ½).
2. Quarter the tomatoes and lay them skin down on a wire rack. Season. Place the wire rack in the oven overnight so the tomatoes dry out.
3. In the morning the tomatoes will be shrivelled and leathery but should still be a little squishy, though not too soft. Put the olive oil into a jar and add the grated garlic, salt and pepper and the capers, if you wish. Push the dried tomatoes into the jar. Cover with more oil, if necessary, and stir well. As long as the tomatoes are under the oil they will not go off as they need air to deteriorate.
4. Store in the fridge for up to 3 months. Do not waste the oil, it is perfect for cooking and salad dressings.

TIP
DRY THESE TOMATOES FOR LESS TIME TO USE IMMEDIATELY – THEY ARE FANTASTIC STIRRED INTO PASTA.

SWEET CAKE TOPPINGS

1. **DRIED FLOWERS** – rose petal, hibiscus and marshmallow flowers are available online. Some fruit teas that are only fruits and not tea leaves will have the same effect. Scatter over cakes.

2. **CHOCOLATE GANACHE** – a grown-up smooth coating or truffle mix. To cover a 20 cm (8 in) cake heat 200 g (7 oz) double cream until nearly boiling, remove from the heat and stir in 200 g (7 oz) chopped dark chocolate until melted. Set aside to cool a little. When it is a thick, coating consistency, pour it over a cake and spread it down the sides with a palette knife. For truffles, leave the mixture until cold, then chill for 4 hours, roll into small balls, then toss in cocoa powder. Or for a fluffy topping, whip the cooling ganache and use to fill and top cakes or it can be piped.

3. **CRUSHED NUT BRITTLE** – praline (see page 85).

4. **VANILLA BUTTERCREAM** – beat 250 g (9 oz/ 2 cups) sifted icing (confectioners') sugar with 150 g (5 oz) room temperature butter, 5 g (¼ oz) vanilla extract and 1 tablespoon water.

5. **CHOCOLATE SPREAD FROSTING** – beat ½ x 400 g (14 oz) jar chocolate spread into the vanilla buttercream recipe above.

6. **BOMBAY BUTTERCREAM** – make the basic vanilla buttercream above but omit the vanilla and water and add the scraped seeds from 3 cardamom pods, 30 g (1 oz) elderflower or ginger and lemongrass cordial, 3 g (⅛ oz) ground turmeric and a few drops of green food colouring (optional).

7   **CREAM CHEESE FROSTING** – great for carrot cakes. See Key Lime Bars on page 108.

8   **TOFFEE BUTTERCREAM** – great for plain or chocolate cakes, see Banoffi Cupcakes on page 31.

9   **MARS BAR ICING** – chop and melt 2 Mars Bars gently in a saucepan with 30 g (1 oz) milk. Add 300 g (10½ oz/2½ cups) sifted icing (confectioners') sugar. Cool until spreadable before use.

10 **SAM'S CHOCOLATE FUDGE ICING** – see Sam's cake on page 46. Brilliant for chocolate cakes but also great for cupcakes.

11 **BERRY BUTTERCREAM** – mix 150 g (5 oz) thawed frozen raspberries or other berries with 100 g (3½ oz/generous ¾ cup) icing (confectioners') sugar and rub through the sieve to make a coulis. Beat 250 g (9 oz/2 cups) sifted icing sugar with 150 g (5 oz) room temperature butter. Gradually beat in the coulis.

12 **CHOCOLATE BUTTERCREAM** – sift 225 g (8 oz/ 1¾ cups) sifted icing (confectioners') sugar and 25 g (1 oz/¼ cup) cocoa powder. Beat into 150 g (5 oz) room temperature butter. Beat in ¼ teaspoon instant coffee dissolved in 30 g (1 oz) cold water.

13 **COFFEE BUTTERCREAM** – beat 250 g (9 oz/ 2 cups) sifted icing (confectioners') sugar with 150 g (5 oz) room temperature butter. Beat in 1 teaspoon instant coffee dissolved in 30 g (1 oz) water.

14 **ROSE FROSTING** – a delicate filling or topping for plain cakes or floral-flavoured cakes. See Rose and Poppy Seed Cake on page 27.

MELTED CHOCOLATE SQUIGGLES AND LETTERS

A great way to personalise a cake or big up its ingredients (see the Chocolate and Beetroot Cake on page 28).

1 Melt some chocolate in a bowl over a saucepan of boiling water. Do not let the bottom of the bowl touch the water, then the heat will not be direct and this will allow the chocolate to melt without burning or splitting. You can do it in a microwave in 30-second bursts, stirring in between melting to make sure it does not burn but you need to keep an eye on it.

2 For squiggles or letters, cover a plate or baking sheet with baking paper. Use a teaspoon and drizzle squiggles or shapes of chocolate over the paper and leave to set. For letters, simply write them as desired. If you make a mistake, just do it again, and if you think one letter is wonky just do that letter again. Alternatively (and more accurately) put the melted chocolate in a disposable piping bag (now available in most shops in the cake baking sections). No need for a nozzle, just snip the end off (close to the tip for thin, or a little further up for thicker). Use the same technique for holding and squeezing the piping bag as described here and pipe squiggles or letters.

PIPING BUTTERCREAM AND TOPPINGS

Use disposable piping bags and a large star nozzle (see Before You Start Cooking, page 8).

1 If you are using a disposable bag, snip the end off the bag so that the fluted edge of the nozzle is protruding out of the end of the bag. Place the bag in a jug and fold the top edges over the jug edges so you can use 2 hands to fill it. Spoon in the prepared buttercream, frosting, whipped ganache or cream. Twist the top of the bag firmly, pushing the topping towards the nozzle. Keep that twist within your grasp so that when you squeeze the bag, the filling is forced down and won't squish out the top. Use your other hand (I use my writing hand for best accuracy) to guide the bag from the tip.

2 To pipe a perfect rosette, hold the nozzle about 2 cm (¾ in) from the top edge of the cake. Squeeze the bag gently so the icing begins to ooze out, pushing towards the cake enough to make the topping stick to the cake, and then draw the bag in a circular motion round the cake, continuing in a spiral towards the centre. Once you have reached the middle, stop squeezing and pull the bag up and away, then you will get a lovely swirl. If you push down slightly when you stop squeezing, you will get a star-shaped blob.

ACKNOWLEDGEMENTS

Special thanks to Lucy Lee-Tirrell for sharing recipes, endless tasting and baking and being such a good friend and good company writing this book. Naomi Hulme for harnessing and coordinating the Skiworld road testers and searching endlessly for the 'perfect recipe' in all her baking for the book. Kate Pollard, my fantastic Publisher and Kajal Mistry, my senior editor at Hardie Grant. Jacqui Melville for her wonderful photography. Leo Greenfield for his lovely illustrations. Emilia Toia for her design work. All the road testers for mixing, beating and baking for this book. And of course Ian, who has tasted every cake in the book, has attempted the first baking of his life for this book and tolerated a 'hectic' kitchen for the last 12 months during the writing of this book – thank you.

ABOUT THE AUTHOR

Lucy trained at the Cordon Bleu School in London before taking up the position of chef to the British Ambassador in Sweden. There she fell in love with skiing and moved to France as head chef in a large ski hotel in Tignes. She made the French Alps her home for the next 15 years cooking for guests in her own ski chalet cooking in the Caribbean and Turkey over the summers.

She has worked as Executive Chef for Skiworld ltd for 10 years, coordinating and creating recipes and menus for over 100 ski chalets all over Europe and North America.

Lucy is managing Director of Lucy's Food that caters for events and parties in Leicestershire and bakes for pubs, cafes and restaurants including Debenham's in store cafes.

She says that if she is not actually cooking then she is either shopping for food, planning food or dreaming about it – a true self confessed foodie. A love she inherited from her mother. Although her heart remains in the mountains she divides her time between London, Leicester and French Alps.

INDEX

Page numbers in *italics* indicate illustrations separated from main recipes.

A

allergies 10
almonds 14 *see also* marzipan
    almond blondies 116–17
    almond thins 68–9
    apple and rye cake 48–9
    fig and almond slab for cheese (pan de higo) 164–5
    Italian citrus & almond cake 44–5
    ricciarelli 92–3
    St Clements cake 32–3
anise seeds
    tortas de aceite 70–1
apples
    apple and cinnamon muffins 62–3
    apple and rye cake 48–9
    Swedish apple cake 34–5

B

baking powder 12
baking tips 8–9
balsamic vinegar 12
    fast balsamic syrup (with variations) 193
bananas 12
    banana and passion fruit cake 64–5
    banoffi cupcakes 30–1
    weird and wonderful banana cake 50–1
banoffi cupcakes 30–1
beer
    Paddy's beer bread 147
beetroot
    chocolate and beetroot cake 28–9
berries
    10-minute berry jam (with variations) 192
    berry and chilli jam 192
    berry and ginger jam 192
biscotti, jewelled 176–7
biscuits & cookies
    almond thins 68–9
    chilli cheese thins 160–1
    classic crunchy biscuits (with variations) 72–3
    coffee and cardamom biscuits 76–7
    digestive biscuits 162, *164*
    homemade hobnobs 75
    mini Marmite bites *169*, 170
    my best ginger snaps 74
    my mum's Viennese biscuits 80–1
    oatcakes 163, *164*
    onion seed and garlic thins *164*, 167
    sesame seed crackers for cheese *164*, 166
    soft cookies (with variations) 78–9
    sour cherry mini florentines 90–1
    tortas de aceite 70–1
Black Forest gâteau for today 60
blackcurrant jam
    Black Forest gâteau for today 60
blueberry and vanilla jam 192
Bombay butterfly cakes 54–5
Bounty biscuits 72–3
bread 132–3
bread making step-by-step 134–5
brioche made simple 136–7
cornbread 157
easy spelt bread 142, *144–5*
lager loaf 156
Paddy's beer bread 147
Parmesan cake 156
picnic loaf 154–5
polenta bread 148–9
potato and onion seed bread 143, *144–5*
seeded wholemeal bread *144–5*, 146
sourdough bread 140–1
sourdough starter 138–9
speedy soda bread 157
tiger tea loaf 152–3
breadcrumbs 44
brioche made simple 136–7
brownies
    Christmas pudding brownies 183
    Lucy's chewy chocolate brownies 122–3
buttercream
    beetroot 28–9
    berry 197
    Bombay 196
    chocolate 197
    coffee 197
    honey 112–13
    passion fruit 64–5
    piping 199
    rosewater & chilli 54–5
    turmeric & ginger 54–5

vanilla **196**
butterfly cakes
   Bombay butterfly cakes **54–5**
   rose and chilli butterfly cakes **54–5**

C

cakes
   15-minute muffins (with variations) **62–3**
   apple and rye cake **48–9**
   banana and passion fruit cake **64–5**
   banoffi cupcakes **30–1**
   Black Forest gâteau for today **60**
   Bombay butterfly cakes **54–5**
   carrot cake **50–1**
   chequerboard cake made easy **58–9**
   chocolate and beetroot cake **28–9**
   chocolate spread cake **36–7**
   Christmas cake **180–1, 184–9**
   dark ginger cake **38–9**
   festive cake decorating **188–9**
   Greek coffee and walnut cake **52–3**
   how to marzipan and flat-ice a rich fruit cake **184–7**
      Italian citrus & almond cake **44–5**
      lemon curd cake **61**
      lemon or orange marzipan cake **56–7**
      Parmesan cake **156**
      parsnip cake **50–1**
      perfect Victoria sandwich cake **40–1**
      plump fruit cake **180–1**
      rose and chilli butterfly cakes **54–5**
      rose and poppy seed cake **26–7**
      Sam's easy chocolate fudge cake **46–7**
      spiced honey cake **24–5**

      St Clements cake **32–3**
      Swedish apple cake **34–5**
      tiger tea loaf **152–3**
      toppings **196–9**
      weird and wonderful banana cake **50–1**
cappuccino biscuits **72–3**
cardamom pods **12**
   coffee and cardamom biscuits **76–7**
carrots
   carrot and walnut muffins **62–3**
   carrot cake **50–1**
cereal bars
   toffee and apricot breakfast bars **120–1**
Cheddar cheese
   mini Marmite bites *169*, **170**
   retro olive bakes *169*, **171**
chequerboard cake made easy **58–9**
cherries
   coloured glacé cherries **12**
   sour cherry and white chocolate muffins **62–3**
   sour cherry mini florentines **90–1**
chestnut purée **12**
   chestnut cups **174–5**
chilli flakes **12**
   berry and chilli jam **192**
   chilli cheese thins **160–1**
   rose and chilli butterfly cakes **54–5**
chocolate **12** *see also* dark chocolate; milk chocolate; white chocolate
   chocolate and beetroot cake **28–9**
   chocolate / double chocolate chip cookies **78–9**
   chocolate fudge icing **46–7**
   chocolate ganache **196**

   chocolate orange cookies **78–9**
   chocolate peppermint creams **97, 99**
   Christmas pudding brownies **183**
   decorating with **198–9**
   double chocolate chip muffins **62–3**
   Hattie's chocolate fudge **86**
   leftover cake truffles **94**
   Lucy's chewy chocolate brownies **122–3**
   Sam's Easter rocky road (with variations) **106–7**
   Sam's easy chocolate fudge cake **46–7**
   specaloo tiffin *107*, **109**
chocolate spread **12**
   chocolate spread cake **36–7**
Christmas cake **180–1, 184–9**
Christmas flapjack **183**
Christmas pudding brownies **183**
cocoa powder **12**
   chocolate fudge icing **46–7**
   Sam's easy chocolate fudge cake **46–7**
coconut
   Daim and coconut cookies **78–9**
   'no-cook' coconut ice **96–7**
coffee
   cappuccino biscuits **72–3**
   coffee and cardamom biscuits **76–7**
   Greek coffee and walnut cake **52–3**
condensed milk **12**
   banoffi cupcakes **30–1**
   key lime bars **108**
   Lottie's loaded bites **119**
   'no-cook' coconut ice **96–7**
   toffee and apricot breakfast bars **120–1**
cornmeal **12**
   cornbread **157**

lemon, cornmeal & rosemary tray 126–7
cranberries
   pink cranberry rocky road 106–7
   white chocolate and cranberry biscuits 72–3
cream cheese
   chocolate spread cake 36–7
   Lucy's chewy chocolate brownies 122–3
cupcakes, banoffi 30–1

D

Daim bars
   Daim and coconut cookies 78–9
   Daim and white chocolate traybake 104–5
dark chocolate
   chestnut cups 174–5
   chocolate and beetroot cake 28–9
   chocolate ganache 196
   dark chocolate and hazelnut biscuits 72–3
   Florentine bars 114–15
   Hattie's chocolate fudge 86
dates 13
   high-energy date bars 128–9
digestive biscuits 162, *164*

E

eggs 13
equipment 11
essences and extracts 13

F

fennel seeds 13
   fennel syrup 193

seeded wholemeal bread *144–5*, 146
fig and almond slab for cheese (pan de higo) 164–5
flapjacks
   Christmas flapjack 183
   honey lavender flapjack 124–5
Florentines
   Florentine bars 114–15
   sour cherry mini Florentines 90–1
flour 13
flowers, dried 196
frosting 197
   chocolate spread frosting 196
   lime frosting 108
   rose frosting 26–7
fruit *see also* individual types
   10-minute berry jam (with variations) 192
fruit, dried
   Florentine bars 114–15
   plump fruit cake 180–1
fudge 88–9
   fudge and Malteser rocky road 106–7
   Hattie's chocolate fudge 86
   oh-so-easy peanut butter fudge 87

G

ginger, crystallised 12
   Bombay butterfly cakes 54–5
   lime chilli and ginger biscuits 72–3
ginger, ground 13, 74
   dark ginger cake 38–9
   my best ginger snaps 74
   parsnip and ginger traybake 112–13
ginger, stem 14

gluten free flour 13
golden syrup 13
gravadlax and beetroot scones 168–9
Greek coffee and walnut cake 52–3

H

hazelnuts
   dark chocolate and hazelnut biscuits 72–3
   jewelled biscotti 176–7
honey 13
   honey lavender flapjack 124–5
   spiced honey cake 24–5
honeycomb rocky road 106–7

I

icing *see also* buttercream; frosting; toppings
   chocolate fudge icing 46–7
   icing, mars bar 197
Italian citrus & almond cake 44–5

J

jams & preserves
   10-minute berry jam (with variations) 192
   foolproof lemon curd 192
   oven-dried tomatoes in garlic oil 194–5
   perfect Victoria sandwich cake 40–1
   preserved lemons 193
jelly bean rocky road 106–7
juniper and gin syrup 193

L

lager loaf 156

lavender 13
   honey lavender flapjack 124–5
   lavender syrup 193
lemons
   foolproof lemon curd 192
   Italian citrus & almond cake 44–5
   lemon, cornmeal & rosemary tray 126–7
   lemon curd cake 61
   lemon drizzle muffins 62–3
   lemon or orange marzipan cake 56–7
   preserved lemons 193
   St Clements cake 32–3
limes 108
   key lime bars *107*, 108
   lime chilli and ginger biscuits 72–3

M

Marmite bites, mini *169*, 170
Mars Bar icing 197
marshmallows
   Lottie's loaded bites *117*, 119
   peanut butter crispy squares 110–11
   Sam's Easter rocky road
      (with variations) 106–7
marzipan 14
   how to marzipan and flat-ice a rich fruit cake 184–7
   lemon or orange marzipan cake 56–7
mascarpone cheese
   Daim and white chocolate traybake
      104–5
mayonnaise 14
   weird and wonderful banana cake 50–1
milk chocolate

Sam's Easter rocky road
   (with variations) 106–7
mincemeat twigs 178–9
muffins, 15-minute (with variations) 62–3

N

nuts
   Florentine bars 114–15
   high-energy date bars 128–9
   nut brittle 84–5
   sour cherry mini florentines 90–1

O

oatcakes 163, *164*
olive bakes, retro *169*, 171
onion seeds 14, 143
   onion seed and garlic thins *164*, 167
   potato and onion seed bread 143, *144–5*
oranges
   chocolate orange cookies 78–9
   Italian citrus & almond cake 44–5
   jewelled biscotti 176–7
   lemon or orange marzipan cake 56–7
   orange and raspberry jam 192
   orange zest and cinnamon biscuits 72–3
   raisin and orange cookies 78–9
   St Clements cake 32–3

P

Parmesan cake 156
parsnips
   parsnip and ginger traybake 112–13
   parsnip cake 50–1
passion fruit 14
   banana and passion fruit cake 64–5

pastries
   mincemeat twigs 178–9
peanut butter
   oh-so-easy peanut butter fudge 87
   peanut butter crispy squares 110–11
   peanut butter jelly bars *117*, 118
peanuts
   Lottie's loaded bites *117*, 119
pears
   Swedish apple cake (variation) 34–5
peppermint creams *97*, 99
picnic loaf 154–5
piping 199
pizza 150–1
polenta bread 148–9
   picnic loaf 154–5
poppy seeds 14
   rose and poppy seed cake 26–7
potato and onion seed bread 143, *144–5*

R

raisin and orange cookies 78–9
Red Leicester cheese
   chilli cheese thins 160–1
ricciarelli 92–3
rice cereal
   peanut butter crispy squares 110–11
rose petals, edible 13, 196
   rose and poppy seed cake 26–7
rose water
   rose and chilli butterfly cakes 54–5
   rose and poppy seed cake 26–7
rye flour
   apple and rye cake 48–9

S

scones, mini savoury (with variations) 168–9
sesame seed crackers for cheese *164*, 166
soda bread 157
sourdough
    sourdough bread 140–1
    sourdough starter 138–9
spelt flour
    easy spelt bread 142, *144–5*
St Clements cake 32–3
stilton and cranberry scones 168–9
strawberry jam, intense 192
sugar 14, 72
Swedish apple cake 34–5
sweets
    chestnut cups 174–5
    Hattie's chocolate fudge 86
    honeycomb 100–1
    leftover cake truffles 94
    'no-cook' coconut ice 96–7
    nut brittle 84–5
    oh-so-easy peanut butter fudge 87
    peppermint creams *97*, 99
    ricciarelli 92–3
    snowball truffles 95
    sour cherry mini florentines 90–1
syrup
    coffee syrup 52–3
    fast balsamic syrup 193
    orange and lemon 44–5

T

tea bread 152–3
tiffin, specaloo *107*, 109
toffee and apricot breakfast bars 120–1
tomatoes
    dried tomatoes and mozzarella scones 168–9
    oven-dried tomatoes in garlic oil 194–5
    tomato and anchovy scones 168–9
toppings 196–8
    piping 199
tortas de aceite 70–1
traybakes
    almond blondies 116–17
    Christmas flapjack 183
    Christmas pudding brownies 183
    Daim and white chocolate traybake 104–5
    fig and almond slab for cheese (pan de higo) 164–5
    Florentine bars 114–15
    high-energy date bars 128–9
    honey lavender flapjack 124–5
    key lime bars *107*, 108
    lemon, cornmeal & rosemary tray 126–7
    Lottie's loaded bites *117*, 119
    Lucy's chewy chocolate brownies 122–3
    parsnip and ginger traybake 112–13
    peanut butter crispy squares 110–11
    peanut butter jelly bars *117*, 118
    Sam's Easter rocky road (with variations) 106–7
    specaloo tiffin *107*, 109
    toffee and apricot breakfast bars 120–1
truffles
    leftover cake truffles 94
    snowball truffles 95
Turkish Delight
    Turkish Delight biscuits 72–3
    Turkish Delight rocky road 106–7
turmeric
    Bombay butterfly cakes 54–5

V

Victoria sandwich
    perfect Victoria sandwich cake 40–1
    Victoria sponge step-by-step 42–3
Viennese biscuits 80–1

W

walnuts
    carrot and walnut muffins 62–3
    Greek coffee and walnut cake 52–3
Werther cookies 78–9
white chocolate
    almond blondies 116–17
    Daim and white chocolate traybake 104–5
    Lottie's loaded bites *117*, 119
    snowball truffles 95
    sour cherry and white chocolate muffins 62–3
    white chocolate and cranberry biscuits 72–3

Y

yeast 14

Lucy's Bakes by Lucy Cufflin

First published in 2015 by Hardie Grant Books

Hardie Grant Books (UK)
Dudley House, North Suite
34–35 Southampton Street
London WC2E 7HF
www.hardiegrant.co.uk

Hardie Grant Books (Australia)
Ground Floor, Building 1
658 Church Street
Melbourne, VIC 3121
www.hardiegrant.com.au

The moral rights of Lucy Cufflin to be identified as the author of this work have been asserted by her in accordance with the Copyright, Designs and Patents Act 1988.

Text © Lucy Cufflin 2015
Photography © Jacqui Melville
Illustrations © Leo Greenfield

All rights reserved. No part of this publication may be reproduced, stored in a retrieval system or transmitted in any form by any means, electronic, electrostatic, magnetic tape, mechanical, photocopying, recording or otherwise, without the prior written permission of the Publisher.

British Library Cataloguing-in-Publication Data. A catalogue record for this book is available from the British Library.

ISBN: 978-174270-937-6

Publisher: Kate Pollard
Senior Editor: Kajal Mistry
Design: Emilia Toia
Photography: © Jacqui Melville
Cover and Internal Illustrations: © Leo Greenfield
Copy Editor: Carolyn Humphries
Proofreaders: Kay Delves and Simon Davis
Indexer: Cathy Heath
Colour Reproduction by p2d

Printed and bound in China by 1010

Find this book on **Cooked.**
Cooked.com.au
Cooked.com

10 9 8 7 6 5 4 3 2 1